Windows Defender Security Center Complete Self-Assessment Guide

The guidance in this Self-Assessment is based on Windows Defender Security Center best practices and standards in business process architecture, design and quality management. The guidance is also based on the professional judgment of the individual collaborators listed in the Acknowledgments.

Notice of rights

You are licensed to use the Self-Assessment contents in your presentations and materials for internal use and customers without asking us - we are here to help.

All rights reserved for the book itself: this book may not be reproduced or transmitted in any form by any means, electronic, mechanical, photocopying, recording, or otherwise, without the prior written permission of the publisher.

The information in this book is distributed on an "As Is" basis without warranty. While every precaution has been taken in the preparation of he book, neither the author nor the publisher shall have any liability to any person or entity with respect to any loss or damage caused or alleged to be caused directly or indirectly by the instructions contained in this book or by the products described in it.

Trademarks

Many of the designations used by manufacturers and sellers to distinguish their products are claimed as trademarks. Where those designations appear in this book, and the publisher was aware of a trademark claim, the designations appear as requested by the owner of the trademark. All other product names and services identified throughout this book are used in editorial fashion only and for the benefit of such companies with no intention of infringement of the trademark. No such use, or the use of any trade name, is intended to convey endorsement or other affiliation with this book.

Copyright © by The Art of Service
http://theartofservice.com
service@theartofservice.com

Table of Contents

About The Art of Service	8
Included Resources - how to access	8
Purpose of this Self-Assessment	10
How to use the Self-Assessment	11
Windows Defender Security Center Scorecard Example	13
Windows Defender Security Center Scorecard	14
BEGINNING OF THE SELF-ASSESSMENT:	15
CRITERION #1: RECOGNIZE	16
CRITERION #2: DEFINE:	28
CRITERION #3: MEASURE:	44
CRITERION #4: ANALYZE:	59
CRITERION #5: IMPROVE:	75
CRITERION #6: CONTROL:	91
CRITERION #7: SUSTAIN:	104
Windows Defender Security Center and Managing Projects, Criteria for Project Managers:	130
1.0 Initiating Process Group: Windows Defender Security Center	131
1.1 Project Charter: Windows Defender Security Center	133
1.2 Stakeholder Register: Windows Defender Security Center	135

1.3 Stakeholder Analysis Matrix: Windows Defender Security Center 136

2.0 Planning Process Group: Windows Defender Security Center 138

2.1 Project Management Plan: Windows Defender Security Center 140

2.2 Scope Management Plan: Windows Defender Security Center 142

2.3 Requirements Management Plan: Windows Defender Security Center 144

2.4 Requirements Documentation: Windows Defender Security Center 146

2.5 Requirements Traceability Matrix: Windows Defender Security Center 148

2.6 Project Scope Statement: Windows Defender Security Center 150

2.7 Assumption and Constraint Log: Windows Defender Security Center 152

2.8 Work Breakdown Structure: Windows Defender Security Center 154

2.9 WBS Dictionary: Windows Defender Security Center 156

2.10 Schedule Management Plan: Windows Defender Security Center 159

2.11 Activity List: Windows Defender Security Center 161

2.12 Activity Attributes: Windows Defender Security Center 163

2.13 Milestone List: Windows Defender Security Center 165

2.14 Network Diagram: Windows Defender Security Center 167

2.15 Activity Resource Requirements: Windows Defender Security Center 169

2.16 Resource Breakdown Structure: Windows Defender Security Center 171

2.17 Activity Duration Estimates: Windows Defender Security Center 173

2.18 Duration Estimating Worksheet: Windows Defender Security Center 175

2.19 Project Schedule: Windows Defender Security Center 177

2.20 Cost Management Plan: Windows Defender Security Center 179

2.21 Activity Cost Estimates: Windows Defender Security Center 181

2.22 Cost Estimating Worksheet: Windows Defender Security Center 183

2.23 Cost Baseline: Windows Defender Security Center 185

2.24 Quality Management Plan: Windows Defender Security Center 187

2.25 Quality Metrics: Windows Defender Security Center 189

2.26 Process Improvement Plan: Windows Defender Security Center   191

2.27 Responsibility Assignment Matrix: Windows Defender Security Center   193

2.28 Roles and Responsibilities: Windows Defender Security Center   195

2.29 Human Resource Management Plan: Windows Defender Security Center   197

2.30 Communications Management Plan: Windows Defender Security Center   199

2.31 Risk Management Plan: Windows Defender Security Center   201

2.32 Risk Register: Windows Defender Security Center   203

2.33 Probability and Impact Assessment: Windows Defender Security Center   205

2.34 Probability and Impact Matrix: Windows Defender Security Center   207

2.35 Risk Data Sheet: Windows Defender Security Center   209

2.36 Procurement Management Plan: Windows Defender Security Center   211

2.37 Source Selection Criteria: Windows Defender Security Center   213

2.38 Stakeholder Management Plan: Windows Defender Security Center   215

2.39 Change Management Plan: Windows Defender Security Center 217

3.0 Executing Process Group: Windows Defender Security Center 219

3.1 Team Member Status Report: Windows Defender Security Center 221

3.2 Change Request: Windows Defender Security Center 223

3.3 Change Log: Windows Defender Security Center 225

3.4 Decision Log: Windows Defender Security Center 227

3.5 Quality Audit: Windows Defender Security Center 229

3.6 Team Directory: Windows Defender Security Center 232

3.7 Team Operating Agreement: Windows Defender Security Center 234

3.8 Team Performance Assessment: Windows Defender Security Center 236

3.9 Team Member Performance Assessment: Windows Defender Security Center 239

3.10 Issue Log: Windows Defender Security Center 241

4.0 Monitoring and Controlling Process Group: Windows Defender Security Center 243

4.1 Project Performance Report: Windows Defender Security Center 245

4.2 Variance Analysis: Windows Defender Security Center 247

4.3 Earned Value Status: Windows Defender Security Center 249

4.4 Risk Audit: Windows Defender Security Center 251

4.5 Contractor Status Report: Windows Defender Security Center 253

4.6 Formal Acceptance: Windows Defender Security Center 255

5.0 Closing Process Group: Windows Defender Security Center 257

5.1 Procurement Audit: Windows Defender Security Center 259

5.2 Contract Close-Out: Windows Defender Security Center 261

5.3 Project or Phase Close-Out: Windows Defender Security Center 263

5.4 Lessons Learned: Windows Defender Security Center 265
Index 268

About The Art of Service

The Art of Service, Business Process Architects since 2000, is dedicated to helping stakeholders achieve excellence.

Defining, designing, creating, and implementing a process to solve a stakeholders challenge or meet an objective is the most valuable role… In EVERY group, company, organization and department.

Unless you're talking a one-time, single-use project, there should be a process. Whether that process is managed and implemented by humans, AI, or a combination of the two, it needs to be designed by someone with a complex enough perspective to ask the right questions.

Someone capable of asking the right questions and step back and say, 'What are we really trying to accomplish here? And is there a different way to look at it?'

With The Art of Service's Standard Requirements Self-Assessments, we empower people who can do just that — whether their title is marketer, entrepreneur, manager, salesperson, consultant, Business Process Manager, executive assistant, IT Manager, CIO etc... —they are the people who rule the future. They are people who watch the process as it happens, and ask the right questions to make the process work better.

Contact us when you need any support with this Self-Assessment and any help with templates, blue-prints and examples of standard documents you might need:

http://theartofservice.com
service@theartofservice.com

Included Resources - how to access

Included with your purchase of the book is the Windows

Defender Security Center Self-Assessment Spreadsheet Dashboard which contains all questions and Self-Assessment areas and auto-generates insights, graphs, and project RACI planning - all with examples to get you started right away.

How? Simply send an email to
access@theartofservice.com
with this books' title in the subject to get the Windows Defender Security Center Self Assessment Tool right away.

You will receive the following contents with New and Updated specific criteria:

- The latest quick edition of the book in PDF

- The latest complete edition of the book in PDF, which criteria correspond to the criteria in...

- The Self-Assessment Excel Dashboard, and...

- Example pre-filled Self-Assessment Excel Dashboard to get familiar with results generation

- In-depth specific Checklists covering the topic

- Project management checklists and templates to assist with implementation

INCLUDES LIFETIME SELF ASSESSMENT UPDATES

Every self assessment comes with Lifetime Updates and Lifetime Free Updated Books. Lifetime Updates is an industry-first feature which allows you to receive verified self assessment updates, ensuring you always have the most accurate information at your fingertips.

Get it now- you will be glad you did - do it now, before you forget.

Send an email to **access@theartofservice.com** with this books' title in the subject to get the Windows Defender Security Center Self Assessment Tool right away.

Purpose of this Self-Assessment

This Self-Assessment has been developed to improve understanding of the requirements and elements of Windows Defender Security Center, based on best practices and standards in business process architecture, design and quality management.

It is designed to allow for a rapid Self-Assessment to determine how closely existing management practices and procedures correspond to the elements of the Self-Assessment.

The criteria of requirements and elements of Windows Defender Security Center have been rephrased in the format of a Self-Assessment questionnaire, with a seven-criterion scoring system, as explained in this document.

In this format, even with limited background knowledge of Windows Defender Security Center, a manager can quickly review existing operations to determine how they measure up to the standards. This in turn can serve as the starting point of a 'gap analysis' to identify management tools or system elements that might usefully be implemented in the organization to help improve overall performance.

How to use the Self-Assessment

On the following pages are a series of questions to identify to what extent your Windows Defender Security Center initiative is complete in comparison to the requirements set in standards.

To facilitate answering the questions, there is a space in front of each question to enter a score on a scale of '1' to '5'.

> 1 Strongly Disagree
>
> 2 Disagree
>
> 3 Neutral
>
> 4 Agree
>
> 5 Strongly Agree

Read the question and rate it with the following in front of mind:

'In my belief, the answer to this question is clearly defined'.

There are two ways in which you can choose to interpret this statement;
1. how aware are you that the answer to the question is clearly defined
2. for more in-depth analysis you can choose to gather evidence and confirm the answer to the question. This obviously will take more time, most Self-Assessment users opt for the first way to interpret the question and dig deeper later on based on the outcome of the overall Self-Assessment.

A score of '1' would mean that the answer is not clear at all, where a '5' would mean the answer is crystal clear and defined. Leave emtpy when the question is not applicable or you don't want to answer it, you can skip it without affecting your score. Write your score in the space provided.

After you have responded to all the appropriate statements in each section, compute your average score for that section, using the formula provided, and round to the nearest tenth. Then transfer to the corresponding spoke in the Windows Defender Security Center Scorecard on the second next page of the Self-Assessment.

Your completed Windows Defender Security Center Scorecard will give you a clear presentation of which Windows Defender Security Center areas need attention.

Windows Defender Security Center Scorecard Example

Example of how the finalized Scorecard can look like:

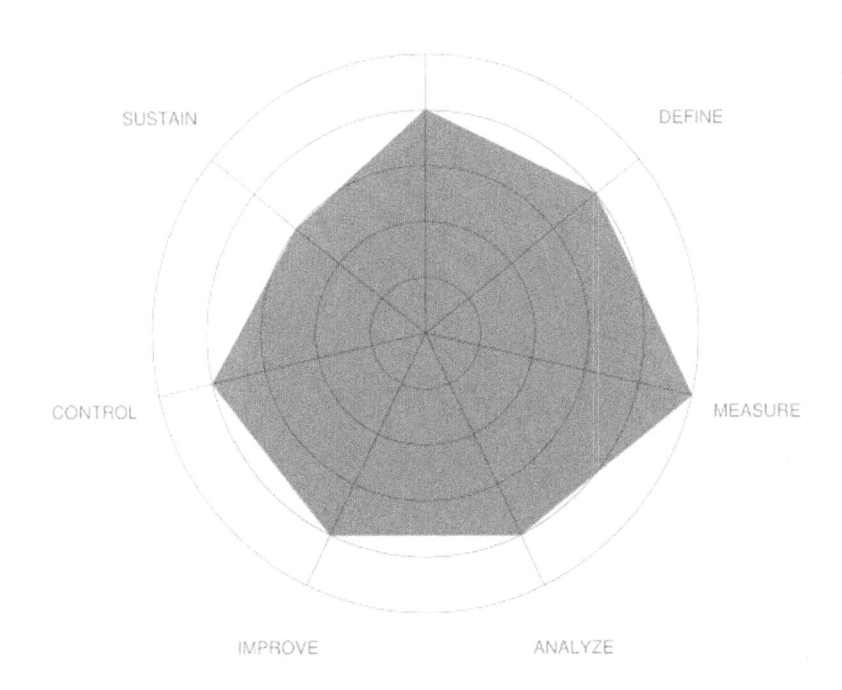

(Radar chart with axes: RECOGNIZE, DEFINE, MEASURE, ANALYZE, IMPROVE, CONTROL, SUSTAIN)

Windows Defender Security Center Scorecard

Your Scores:

RECOGNIZE

SUSTAIN

DEFINE

CONTROL

MEASURE

IMPROVE

ANALYZE

**BEGINNING OF THE
SELF-ASSESSMENT:**

CRITERION #1: RECOGNIZE

INTENT: Be aware of the need for change. Recognize that there is an unfavorable variation, problem or symptom.

In my belief, the answer to this question is clearly defined:

5 Strongly Agree

4 Agree

3 Neutral

2 Disagree

1 Strongly Disagree

1. Why is this needed?
<--- Score

2. Does Windows Defender Security Center create potential expectations in other areas that need to be recognized and considered?
<--- Score

3. What Windows Defender Security Center

capabilities do you need?
<--- Score

4. What is the problem or issue?
<--- Score

5. Are there Windows Defender Security Center problems defined?
<--- Score

6. How does it fit into your organizational needs and tasks?
<--- Score

7. What vendors make products that address the Windows Defender Security Center needs?
<--- Score

8. Is it needed?
<--- Score

9. Are problem definition and motivation clearly presented?
<--- Score

10. Who else hopes to benefit from it?
<--- Score

11. To what extent would your organization benefit from being recognized as a award recipient?
<--- Score

12. Does your organization need more Windows Defender Security Center education?
<--- Score

13. What situation(s) led to this Windows Defender Security Center Self Assessment?

<--- Score

14. What training and capacity building actions are needed to implement proposed reforms?

<--- Score

15. Is it clear when you think of the day ahead of you what activities and tasks you need to complete?

<--- Score

16. As a sponsor, customer or management, how important is it to meet goals, objectives?

<--- Score

17. Do you need to avoid or amend any Windows Defender Security Center activities?

<--- Score

18. Are there recognized Windows Defender Security Center problems?

<--- Score

19. Who needs budgets?

<--- Score

20. Who needs to know?

<--- Score

21. Who needs what information?

<--- Score

22. Have you identified your Windows Defender Security Center key performance indicators?

<--- Score

23. What Windows Defender Security Center coordination do you need?
<--- Score

24. What are the clients issues and concerns?
<--- Score

25. Would you recognize a threat from the inside?
<--- Score

26. Is the quality assurance team identified?
<--- Score

27. Will a response program recognize when a crisis occurs and provide some level of response?
<--- Score

28. When a Windows Defender Security Center manager recognizes a problem, what options are available?
<--- Score

29. Are there any specific expectations or concerns about the Windows Defender Security Center team, Windows Defender Security Center itself?
<--- Score

30. Will Windows Defender Security Center deliverables need to be tested and, if so, by whom?
<--- Score

31. Are employees recognized for desired behaviors?
<--- Score

32. Are you dealing with any of the same issues today as yesterday? What can you do about this?
<--- Score

33. What creative shifts do you need to take?
<--- Score

34. What is the extent or complexity of the Windows Defender Security Center problem?
<--- Score

35. How do you take a forward-looking perspective in identifying Windows Defender Security Center research related to market response and models?
<--- Score

36. Whom do you really need or want to serve?
<--- Score

37. Consider your own Windows Defender Security Center project, what types of organizational problems do you think might be causing or affecting your problem, based on the work done so far?
<--- Score

38. Are controls defined to recognize and contain problems?
<--- Score

39. What do employees need in the short term?
<--- Score

40. Who needs to know about Windows Defender Security Center?
<--- Score

41. What are the minority interests and what amount of minority interests can be recognized?
<--- Score

42. How are you going to measure success?
<--- Score

43. Which needs are not included or involved?
<--- Score

44. Who defines the rules in relation to any given issue?
<--- Score

45. For your Windows Defender Security Center project, identify and describe the business environment, is there more than one layer to the business environment?
<--- Score

46. What needs to stay?
<--- Score

47. Do you recognize Windows Defender Security Center achievements?
<--- Score

48. How do you identify subcontractor relationships?
<--- Score

49. To what extent does each concerned units management team recognize Windows Defender Security Center as an effective investment?
<--- Score

50. How do you recognize an Windows Defender

Security Center objection?
<--- Score

51. Who are your key stakeholders who need to sign off?
<--- Score

52. Think about the people you identified for your Windows Defender Security Center project and the project responsibilities you would assign to them, what kind of training do you think they would need to perform these responsibilities effectively?
<--- Score

53. What are the stakeholder objectives to be achieved with Windows Defender Security Center?
<--- Score

54. Which information does the Windows Defender Security Center business case need to include?
<--- Score

55. Do you need different information or graphics?
<--- Score

56. What problems are you facing and how do you consider Windows Defender Security Center will circumvent those obstacles?
<--- Score

57. What resources or support might you need?
<--- Score

58. What are your needs in relation to Windows Defender Security Center skills, labor, equipment, and markets?

<--- Score

59. What is the recognized need?
<--- Score

60. Is the need for organizational change recognized?
<--- Score

61. What does Windows Defender Security Center success mean to the stakeholders?
<--- Score

62. How are the Windows Defender Security Center's objectives aligned to the group's overall stakeholder strategy?
<--- Score

63. How do you identify the kinds of information that you will need?
<--- Score

64. What are the timeframes required to resolve each of the issues/problems?
<--- Score

65. Do you know what you need to know about Windows Defender Security Center?
<--- Score

66. How are training requirements identified?
<--- Score

67. Where do you need to exercise leadership?
<--- Score

68. What is the smallest subset of the problem you can usefully solve?
<--- Score

69. How can auditing be a preventative security measure?
<--- Score

70. Are losses recognized in a timely manner?
<--- Score

71. Are there regulatory / compliance issues?
<--- Score

72. Are there any revenue recognition issues?
<--- Score

73. What tools and technologies are needed for a custom Windows Defender Security Center project?
<--- Score

74. What Windows Defender Security Center problem should be solved?
<--- Score

75. What do you need to start doing?
<--- Score

76. How many trainings, in total, are needed?
<--- Score

77. What would happen if Windows Defender Security Center weren't done?
<--- Score

78. Does the problem have ethical dimensions?

<--- Score

79. What else needs to be measured?
<--- Score

80. What prevents you from making the changes you know will make you a more effective Windows Defender Security Center leader?
<--- Score

81. How do you recognize an objection?
<--- Score

82. What activities does the governance board need to consider?
<--- Score

83. Where is training needed?
<--- Score

84. Did you miss any major Windows Defender Security Center issues?
<--- Score

85. What extra resources will you need?
<--- Score

86. Can management personnel recognize the monetary benefit of Windows Defender Security Center?
<--- Score

87. What information do users need?
<--- Score

88. Why the need?

<--- Score

89. Do you have/need 24-hour access to key personnel?
<--- Score

90. Which issues are too important to ignore?
<--- Score

91. Are your goals realistic? Do you need to redefine your problem? Perhaps the problem has changed or maybe you have reached your goal and need to set a new one?
<--- Score

92. How much are sponsors, customers, partners, stakeholders involved in Windows Defender Security Center? In other words, what are the risks, if Windows Defender Security Center does not deliver successfully?
<--- Score

93. What is the Windows Defender Security Center problem definition? What do you need to resolve?
<--- Score

94. Looking at each person individually – does every one have the qualities which are needed to work in this group?
<--- Score

95. What Windows Defender Security Center events should you attend?
<--- Score

96. What are the Windows Defender Security Center

resources needed?
<--- Score

97. What are the expected benefits of Windows Defender Security Center to the stakeholder?
<--- Score

Add up total points for this section:
_____ = Total points for this section

Divided by: _____ (number of statements answered) = _____
Average score for this section

Transfer your score to the Windows Defender Security Center Index at the beginning of the Self-Assessment.

CRITERION #2: DEFINE:

INTENT: Formulate the stakeholder problem. Define the problem, needs and objectives.

In my belief, the answer to this question is clearly defined:

5 Strongly Agree

4 Agree

3 Neutral

2 Disagree

1 Strongly Disagree

1. Has anyone else (internal or external to the group) attempted to solve this problem or a similar one before? If so, what knowledge can be leveraged from these previous efforts?
<--- Score

2. How often are the team meetings?
<--- Score

3. What are the compelling stakeholder reasons for embarking on Windows Defender Security Center?
<--- Score

4. What happens if Windows Defender Security Center's scope changes?
<--- Score

5. Will a Windows Defender Security Center production readiness review be required?
<--- Score

6. What constraints exist that might impact the team?
<--- Score

7. How do you think the partners involved in Windows Defender Security Center would have defined success?
<--- Score

8. What are the Windows Defender Security Center use cases?
<--- Score

9. What is the context?
<--- Score

10. Has the Windows Defender Security Center work been fairly and/or equitably divided and delegated among team members who are qualified and capable to perform the work? Has everyone contributed?
<--- Score

11. Are there different segments of customers?
<--- Score

12. If substitutes have been appointed, have they been briefed on the Windows Defender Security Center goals and received regular communications as to the progress to date?
<--- Score

13. How have you defined all Windows Defender Security Center requirements first?
<--- Score

14. Has a high-level 'as is' process map been completed, verified and validated?
<--- Score

15. Are resources adequate for the scope?
<--- Score

16. Is the team adequately staffed with the desired cross-functionality? If not, what additional resources are available to the team?
<--- Score

17. Is Windows Defender Security Center required?
<--- Score

18. Are the Windows Defender Security Center requirements testable?
<--- Score

19. What sources do you use to gather information for a Windows Defender Security Center study?
<--- Score

20. Have all of the relationships been defined properly?
<--- Score

21. What information should you gather?
<--- Score

22. Is the Windows Defender Security Center scope manageable?
<--- Score

23. What specifically is the problem? Where does it occur? When does it occur? What is its extent?
<--- Score

24. What are the requirements for audit information?
<--- Score

25. What Windows Defender Security Center services do you require?
<--- Score

26. Is scope creep really all bad news?
<--- Score

27. What intelligence can you gather?
<--- Score

28. Is there any additional Windows Defender Security Center definition of success?
<--- Score

29. Is the Windows Defender Security Center scope complete and appropriately sized?
<--- Score

30. How do you keep key subject matter experts in the loop?
<--- Score

31. Who is gathering Windows Defender Security Center information?

<--- Score

32. How will the Windows Defender Security Center team and the group measure complete success of Windows Defender Security Center?
<--- Score

33. What baselines are required to be defined and managed?
<--- Score

34. Does the team have regular meetings?
<--- Score

35. Are accountability and ownership for Windows Defender Security Center clearly defined?

<--- Score

36. Do you have organizational privacy requirements?
<--- Score

37. Is the work to date meeting requirements?
<--- Score

38. What are (control) requirements for Windows Defender Security Center Information?

<--- Score

39. How do you catch Windows Defender Security Center definition inconsistencies?

<--- Score

40. Has a Windows Defender Security Center

requirement not been met?
<--- Score

41. What are the Roles and Responsibilities for each team member and its leadership? Where is this documented?
<--- Score

42. What system do you use for gathering Windows Defender Security Center information?
<--- Score

43. Is Windows Defender Security Center linked to key stakeholder goals and objectives?
<--- Score

44. How is the team tracking and documenting its work?
<--- Score

45. How do you manage unclear Windows Defender Security Center requirements?
<--- Score

46. What is the scope of Windows Defender Security Center?
<--- Score

47. When are meeting minutes sent out? Who is on the distribution list?
<--- Score

48. What information do you gather?
<--- Score

49. How can the value of Windows Defender Security

Center be defined?
<--- Score

50. Are audit criteria, scope, frequency and methods defined?
<--- Score

51. Who approved the Windows Defender Security Center scope?
<--- Score

52. What scope to assess?
<--- Score

53. How do you build the right business case?
<--- Score

54. Are roles and responsibilities formally defined?
<--- Score

55. What gets examined?
<--- Score

56. How do you manage changes in Windows Defender Security Center requirements?
<--- Score

57. Have specific policy objectives been defined?
<--- Score

58. Has/have the customer(s) been identified?
<--- Score

59. How will variation in the actual durations of each activity be dealt with to ensure that the expected Windows Defender Security Center results are met?

<--- Score

60. How do you manage scope?
<--- Score

61. Have the customer needs been translated into specific, measurable requirements? How?
<--- Score

62. Have all basic functions of Windows Defender Security Center been defined?
<--- Score

63. Are different versions of process maps needed to account for the different types of inputs?
<--- Score

64. Scope of sensitive information?
<--- Score

65. Do you all define Windows Defender Security Center in the same way?
<--- Score

66. What scope do you want your strategy to cover?
<--- Score

67. What customer feedback methods were used to solicit their input?
<--- Score

68. Where can you gather more information?
<--- Score

69. How do you hand over Windows Defender Security Center context?

<--- Score

70. What is the worst case scenario?
<--- Score

71. How do you gather Windows Defender Security Center requirements?
<--- Score

72. How do you gather the stories?
<--- Score

73. How do you gather requirements?
<--- Score

74. The political context: who holds power?
<--- Score

75. Are the Windows Defender Security Center requirements complete?
<--- Score

76. Is it clearly defined in and to your organization what you do?
<--- Score

77. What is the definition of success?
<--- Score

78. Is special Windows Defender Security Center user knowledge required?
<--- Score

79. What is the scope of the Windows Defender Security Center effort?
<--- Score

80. Does the scope remain the same?
<--- Score

81. What was the context?
<--- Score

82. Is there a critical path to deliver Windows Defender Security Center results?
<--- Score

83. Do the problem and goal statements meet the SMART criteria (specific, measurable, attainable, relevant, and time-bound)?
<--- Score

84. In what way can you redefine the criteria of choice clients have in your category in your favor?
<--- Score

85. What are the dynamics of the communication plan?
<--- Score

86. How would you define the culture at your organization, how susceptible is it to Windows Defender Security Center changes?
<--- Score

87. Is the scope of Windows Defender Security Center defined?
<--- Score

88. Has everyone on the team, including the team leaders, been properly trained?
<--- Score

89. What Windows Defender Security Center requirements should be gathered?
<--- Score

90. Has a team charter been developed and communicated?
<--- Score

91. What is out-of-scope initially?
<--- Score

92. Is the improvement team aware of the different versions of a process: what they think it is vs. what it actually is vs. what it should be vs. what it could be?
<--- Score

93. Who is gathering information?
<--- Score

94. When is/was the Windows Defender Security Center start date?
<--- Score

95. What critical content must be communicated – who, what, when, where, and how?
<--- Score

96. What defines best in class?
<--- Score

97. What are the record-keeping requirements of Windows Defender Security Center activities?
<--- Score

98. What is the scope of the Windows Defender

Security Center work?
<--- Score

99. What is in the scope and what is not in scope?
<--- Score

100. How does the Windows Defender Security Center manager ensure against scope creep?
<--- Score

101. What is a worst-case scenario for losses?
<--- Score

102. Are task requirements clearly defined?
<--- Score

103. What is out of scope?
<--- Score

104. What sort of initial information to gather?
<--- Score

105. How would you define Windows Defender Security Center leadership?
<--- Score

106. What are the tasks and definitions?
<--- Score

107. Has a project plan, Gantt chart, or similar been developed/completed?
<--- Score

108. Why are you doing Windows Defender Security Center and what is the scope?
<--- Score

109. How was the 'as is' process map developed, reviewed, verified and validated?
<--- Score

110. What are the core elements of the Windows Defender Security Center business case?
<--- Score

111. Are there any constraints known that bear on the ability to perform Windows Defender Security Center work? How is the team addressing them?
<--- Score

112. Who defines (or who defined) the rules and roles?
<--- Score

113. What are the boundaries of the scope? What is in bounds and what is not? What is the start point? What is the stop point?
<--- Score

114. What key stakeholder process output measure(s) does Windows Defender Security Center leverage and how?
<--- Score

115. What are the Windows Defender Security Center tasks and definitions?
<--- Score

116. What is the definition of Windows Defender Security Center excellence?
<--- Score

117. Is there a clear Windows Defender Security

Center case definition?
<--- Score

118. What is the scope?
<--- Score

119. Are approval levels defined for contracts and supplements to contracts?
<--- Score

120. Has your scope been defined?
<--- Score

121. What would be the goal or target for a Windows Defender Security Center's improvement team?
<--- Score

122. Are all requirements met?
<--- Score

123. Is there regularly 100% attendance at the team meetings? If not, have appointed substitutes attended to preserve cross-functionality and full representation?
<--- Score

124. How did the Windows Defender Security Center manager receive input to the development of a Windows Defender Security Center improvement plan and the estimated completion dates/times of each activity?
<--- Score

125. How are consistent Windows Defender Security Center definitions important?
<--- Score

126. When is the estimated completion date?
<--- Score

127. Are required metrics defined, what are they?
<--- Score

128. What are the rough order estimates on cost savings/opportunities that Windows Defender Security Center brings?
<--- Score

129. Has the direction changed at all during the course of Windows Defender Security Center? If so, when did it change and why?
<--- Score

130. Is Windows Defender Security Center currently on schedule according to the plan?
<--- Score

131. What is in scope?
<--- Score

132. Is the current 'as is' process being followed? If not, what are the discrepancies?
<--- Score

133. Has the improvement team collected the 'voice of the customer' (obtained feedback – qualitative and quantitative)?
<--- Score

134. Do you have a Windows Defender Security Center success story or case study ready to tell and share?

<--- Score

Add up total points for this section:
_____ = Total points for this section

Divided by: _____ (number of statements answered) = _____
Average score for this section

Transfer your score to the Windows Defender Security Center Index at the beginning of the Self-Assessment.

CRITERION #3: MEASURE:

INTENT: Gather the correct data. Measure the current performance and evolution of the situation.

In my belief, the answer to this question is clearly defined:

5 Strongly Agree

4 Agree

3 Neutral

2 Disagree

1 Strongly Disagree

1. How do you verify and develop ideas and innovations?
<--- Score

2. What causes investor action?
<--- Score

3. How do you measure success?
<--- Score

4. Are the Windows Defender Security Center benefits worth its costs?
<--- Score

5. How will costs be allocated?
<--- Score

6. What is the total fixed cost?
<--- Score

7. Are you able to realize any cost savings?
<--- Score

8. How can you measure Windows Defender Security Center in a systematic way?
<--- Score

9. How do you measure efficient delivery of Windows Defender Security Center services?
<--- Score

10. How to cause the change?
<--- Score

11. What are the Windows Defender Security Center key cost drivers?
<--- Score

12. What is the root cause(s) of the problem?
<--- Score

13. Are you aware of what could cause a problem?
<--- Score

14. What are the strategic priorities for this year?

<--- Score

15. How do you prevent mis-estimating cost?
<--- Score

16. What are the costs of delaying Windows Defender Security Center action?
<--- Score

17. Are there any easy-to-implement alternatives to Windows Defender Security Center? Sometimes other solutions are available that do not require the cost implications of a full-blown project?
<--- Score

18. Does management have the right priorities among projects?
<--- Score

19. How do you aggregate measures across priorities?
<--- Score

20. Does a Windows Defender Security Center quantification method exist?
<--- Score

21. Is the cost worth the Windows Defender Security Center effort ?
<--- Score

22. Do you effectively measure and reward individual and team performance?
<--- Score

23. What are the costs?

<--- Score

24. How are measurements made?
<--- Score

25. How do you measure lifecycle phases?
<--- Score

26. Where is it measured?
<--- Score

27. What are the Windows Defender Security Center investment costs?
<--- Score

28. Is it possible to estimate the impact of unanticipated complexity such as wrong or failed assumptions, feedback, etcetera on proposed reforms?
<--- Score

29. What are the current costs of the Windows Defender Security Center process?
<--- Score

30. What users will be impacted?
<--- Score

31. How can a Windows Defender Security Center test verify your ideas or assumptions?
<--- Score

32. Who should receive measurement reports?
<--- Score

33. Have you made assumptions about the shape of

the future, particularly its impact on your customers and competitors?

<--- Score

34. How can you reduce costs?

<--- Score

35. How sensitive must the Windows Defender Security Center strategy be to cost?

<--- Score

36. What does losing customers cost your organization?

<--- Score

37. What disadvantage does this cause for the user?

<--- Score

38. What measurements are being captured?

<--- Score

39. What is measured? Why?

<--- Score

40. Where is the cost?

<--- Score

41. How do you verify your resources?

<--- Score

42. Are supply costs steady or fluctuating?

<--- Score

43. What would be a real cause for concern?

<--- Score

44. How do you verify and validate the Windows Defender Security Center data?
<--- Score

45. Among the Windows Defender Security Center product and service cost to be estimated, which is considered hardest to estimate?
<--- Score

46. Are the units of measure consistent?
<--- Score

47. Are the measurements objective?
<--- Score

48. How can you manage cost down?
<--- Score

49. What evidence is there and what is measured?
<--- Score

50. Where can you go to verify the info?
<--- Score

51. How do you quantify and qualify impacts?
<--- Score

52. What is the total cost related to deploying Windows Defender Security Center, including any consulting or professional services?
<--- Score

53. What tests verify requirements?
<--- Score

54. What are allowable costs?

<--- Score

55. What drives O&M cost?
<--- Score

56. Are there measurements based on task performance?
<--- Score

57. Are Windows Defender Security Center vulnerabilities categorized and prioritized?
<--- Score

58. How do you verify if Windows Defender Security Center is built right?
<--- Score

59. Are missed Windows Defender Security Center opportunities costing your organization money?
<--- Score

60. What could cause you to change course?
<--- Score

61. What is the cost of rework?
<--- Score

62. How is the value delivered by Windows Defender Security Center being measured?
<--- Score

63. Do you have a flow diagram of what happens?
<--- Score

64. What happens if cost savings do not materialize?
<--- Score

65. How can you measure the performance?
<--- Score

66. What details are required of the Windows Defender Security Center cost structure?
<--- Score

67. How is performance measured?
<--- Score

68. What would it cost to replace your technology?
<--- Score

69. Do you have any cost Windows Defender Security Center limitation requirements?
<--- Score

70. Have design-to-cost goals been established?
<--- Score

71. Are you taking your company in the direction of better and revenue or cheaper and cost?
<--- Score

72. What could cause delays in the schedule?
<--- Score

73. How do you verify performance?
<--- Score

74. At what cost?
<--- Score

75. Is there an opportunity to verify requirements?
<--- Score

76. How are costs allocated?
<--- Score

77. How will you measure success?
<--- Score

78. What is the cause of any Windows Defender Security Center gaps?
<--- Score

79. What are the costs and benefits?
<--- Score

80. Which Windows Defender Security Center impacts are significant?
<--- Score

81. What causes mismanagement?
<--- Score

82. What methods are feasible and acceptable to estimate the impact of reforms?
<--- Score

83. How much does it cost?
<--- Score

84. Was a business case (cost/benefit) developed?
<--- Score

85. Do the benefits outweigh the costs?
<--- Score

86. How is progress measured?
<--- Score

87. Have you included everything in your Windows Defender Security Center cost models?
<--- Score

88. How do you verify the Windows Defender Security Center requirements quality?
<--- Score

89. Did you tackle the cause or the symptom?
<--- Score

90. What are your primary costs, revenues, assets?
<--- Score

91. How will effects be measured?
<--- Score

92. What are your operating costs?
<--- Score

93. What does a Test Case verify?
<--- Score

94. What are your key Windows Defender Security Center organizational performance measures, including key short and longer-term financial measures?
<--- Score

95. Do you have an issue in getting priority?
<--- Score

96. When should you bother with diagrams?
<--- Score

97. What harm might be caused?

<--- Score

98. What potential environmental factors impact the Windows Defender Security Center effort?

<--- Score

99. How do you measure variability?

<--- Score

100. When a disaster occurs, who gets priority?

<--- Score

101. How can you reduce the costs of obtaining inputs?

<--- Score

102. What are the uncertainties surrounding estimates of impact?

<--- Score

103. How long to keep data and how to manage retention costs?

<--- Score

104. What is an unallowable cost?

<--- Score

105. How will success or failure be measured?

<--- Score

106. What do people want to verify?

<--- Score

107. What are hidden Windows Defender Security Center quality costs?

54

<--- Score

108. Which measures and indicators matter?
<--- Score

109. How do your measurements capture actionable Windows Defender Security Center information for use in exceeding your customers expectations and securing your customers engagement?
<--- Score

110. Has a cost center been established?
<--- Score

111. What are your customers expectations and measures?
<--- Score

112. Which costs should be taken into account?
<--- Score

113. What are the types and number of measures to use?
<--- Score

114. What causes extra work or rework?
<--- Score

115. When are costs are incurred?
<--- Score

116. Do you aggressively reward and promote the people who have the biggest impact on creating excellent Windows Defender Security Center services/products?
<--- Score

117. How frequently do you track Windows Defender Security Center measures?
<--- Score

118. Why do the measurements/indicators matter?
<--- Score

119. What are the costs of reform?
<--- Score

120. What is your Windows Defender Security Center quality cost segregation study?
<--- Score

121. What relevant entities could be measured?
<--- Score

122. What are the estimated costs of proposed changes?
<--- Score

123. Will Windows Defender Security Center have an impact on current business continuity, disaster recovery processes and/or infrastructure?
<--- Score

124. What do you measure and why?
<--- Score

125. What are you verifying?
<--- Score

126. What causes innovation to fail or succeed in your organization?
<--- Score

127. What is the Windows Defender Security Center business impact?
<--- Score

128. Are actual costs in line with budgeted costs?
<--- Score

129. What does your operating model cost?
<--- Score

130. What is your decision requirements diagram?
<--- Score

131. What are the operational costs after Windows Defender Security Center deployment?
<--- Score

132. How will your organization measure success?
<--- Score

133. Is the solution cost-effective?
<--- Score

134. How do you control the overall costs of your work processes?
<--- Score

135. What measurements are possible, practicable and meaningful?
<--- Score

Add up total points for this section:
_____ = Total points for this section

Divided by: _____ (number of

statements answered) = _____
Average score for this section

Transfer your score to the Windows Defender Security Center Index at the beginning of the Self-Assessment.

CRITERION #4: ANALYZE:

INTENT: Analyze causes, assumptions and hypotheses.

In my belief, the answer to this question is clearly defined:

5 Strongly Agree

4 Agree

3 Neutral

2 Disagree

1 Strongly Disagree

1. Was a cause-and-effect diagram used to explore the different types of causes (or sources of variation)?
<--- Score

2. What are evaluation criteria for the output?
<--- Score

3. What are your Windows Defender Security Center processes?
<--- Score

4. Do your contracts/agreements contain data security obligations?
<--- Score

5. Think about the functions involved in your Windows Defender Security Center project, what processes flow from these functions?
<--- Score

6. What data do you need to collect?
<--- Score

7. What qualifications do Windows Defender Security Center leaders need?
<--- Score

8. How do you define collaboration and team output?
<--- Score

9. How do you ensure that the Windows Defender Security Center opportunity is realistic?
<--- Score

10. What training and qualifications will you need?
<--- Score

11. What is the cost of poor quality as supported by the team's analysis?
<--- Score

12. Were Pareto charts (or similar) used to portray the 'heavy hitters' (or key sources of variation)?
<--- Score

13. Is there any way to speed up the process?

<--- Score

14. Are your outputs consistent?
<--- Score

15. Is the required Windows Defender Security Center data gathered?
<--- Score

16. Who will gather what data?
<--- Score

17. What qualifications and skills do you need?
<--- Score

18. Have any additional benefits been identified that will result from closing all or most of the gaps?
<--- Score

19. What, related to, Windows Defender Security Center processes does your organization outsource?
<--- Score

20. What kind of crime could a potential new hire have committed that would not only not disqualify him/her from being hired by your organization, but would actually indicate that he/she might be a particularly good fit?
<--- Score

21. Is pre-qualification of suppliers carried out?
<--- Score

22. How do you use Windows Defender Security Center data and information to support

organizational decision making and innovation?
<--- Score

23. What are the personnel training and qualifications required?
<--- Score

24. What process should you select for improvement?
<--- Score

25. Think about some of the processes you undertake within your organization, which do you own?
<--- Score

26. Where is Windows Defender Security Center data gathered?
<--- Score

27. What are the Windows Defender Security Center design outputs?
<--- Score

28. What quality tools were used to get through the analyze phase?
<--- Score

29. Is the Windows Defender Security Center process severely broken such that a re-design is necessary?
<--- Score

30. How is the way you as the leader think and process information affecting your organizational culture?
<--- Score

31. Who is involved in the management review process?

<--- Score

32. Do quality systems drive continuous improvement?
<--- Score

33. Who owns what data?
<--- Score

34. What internal processes need improvement?
<--- Score

35. How often will data be collected for measures?
<--- Score

36. What other organizational variables, such as reward systems or communication systems, affect the performance of this Windows Defender Security Center process?
<--- Score

37. What are your outputs?
<--- Score

38. How is data used for program management and improvement?
<--- Score

39. Do several people in different organizational units assist with the Windows Defender Security Center process?
<--- Score

40. How difficult is it to qualify what Windows Defender Security Center ROI is?
<--- Score

41. What is the Value Stream Mapping?
<--- Score

42. How do you promote understanding that opportunity for improvement is not criticism of the status quo, or the people who created the status quo?
<--- Score

43. How is the Windows Defender Security Center Value Stream Mapping managed?
<--- Score

44. Do your employees have the opportunity to do what they do best everyday?
<--- Score

45. Is data and process analysis, root cause analysis and quantifying the gap/opportunity in place?
<--- Score

46. What is the complexity of the output produced?
<--- Score

47. Where is the data coming from to measure compliance?
<--- Score

48. How can risk management be tied procedurally to process elements?
<--- Score

49. What is the output?
<--- Score

50. Is there an established change management process?
<--- Score

51. Has an output goal been set?
<--- Score

52. What qualifications are necessary?
<--- Score

53. What resources go in to get the desired output?
<--- Score

54. What tools were used to generate the list of possible causes?
<--- Score

55. How do you identify specific Windows Defender Security Center investment opportunities and emerging trends?
<--- Score

56. What Windows Defender Security Center data will be collected?
<--- Score

57. An organizationally feasible system request is one that considers the mission, goals and objectives of the organization, key questions are: is the Windows Defender Security Center solution request practical and will it solve a problem or take advantage of an opportunity to achieve company goals?
<--- Score

58. Identify an operational issue in your organization,

for example, could a particular task be done more quickly or more efficiently by Windows Defender Security Center?

<--- Score

59. How has the Windows Defender Security Center data been gathered?

<--- Score

60. What do you need to qualify?

<--- Score

61. What are your current levels and trends in key measures or indicators of Windows Defender Security Center product and process performance that are important to and directly serve your customers? How do these results compare with the performance of your competitors and other organizations with similar offerings?

<--- Score

62. Do staff qualifications match your project?

<--- Score

63. What other jobs or tasks affect the performance of the steps in the Windows Defender Security Center process?

<--- Score

64. Do your leaders quickly bounce back from setbacks?

<--- Score

65. Should you invest in industry-recognized qualifications?

<--- Score

66. What qualifications are needed?
<--- Score

67. What does the data say about the performance of the stakeholder process?
<--- Score

68. Can you add value to the current Windows Defender Security Center decision-making process (largely qualitative) by incorporating uncertainty modeling (more quantitative)?
<--- Score

69. What are the necessary qualifications?
<--- Score

70. Is the suppliers process defined and controlled?
<--- Score

71. What information qualified as important?
<--- Score

72. What qualifies as competition?
<--- Score

73. How do mission and objectives affect the Windows Defender Security Center processes of your organization?
<--- Score

74. What process improvements will be needed?
<--- Score

75. Was a detailed process map created to amplify critical steps of the 'as is' stakeholder process?

<--- Score

76. What is the Windows Defender Security Center Driver?

<--- Score

77. What Windows Defender Security Center metrics are outputs of the process?

<--- Score

78. How will the data be checked for quality?

<--- Score

79. What are the revised rough estimates of the financial savings/opportunity for Windows Defender Security Center improvements?

<--- Score

80. Has data output been validated?

<--- Score

81. How does the organization define, manage, and improve its Windows Defender Security Center processes?

<--- Score

82. What were the crucial 'moments of truth' on the process map?

<--- Score

83. Do you have the authority to produce the output?

<--- Score

84. Are gaps between current performance and the goal performance identified?

<--- Score

85. What are the disruptive Windows Defender Security Center technologies that enable your organization to radically change your business processes?
<--- Score

86. Is the gap/opportunity displayed and communicated in financial terms?
<--- Score

87. Are you missing Windows Defender Security Center opportunities?
<--- Score

88. Are all staff in core Windows Defender Security Center subjects Highly Qualified?
<--- Score

89. Record-keeping requirements flow from the records needed as inputs, outputs, controls and for transformation of a Windows Defender Security Center process, are the records needed as inputs to the Windows Defender Security Center process available?
<--- Score

90. How do you measure the operational performance of your key work systems and processes, including productivity, cycle time, and other appropriate measures of process effectiveness, efficiency, and innovation?
<--- Score

91. What tools were used to narrow the list of possible

causes?
<--- Score

92. How will the Windows Defender Security Center data be captured?
<--- Score

93. How is Windows Defender Security Center data gathered?
<--- Score

94. What are the Windows Defender Security Center business drivers?
<--- Score

95. When should a process be art not science?
<--- Score

96. What data is gathered?
<--- Score

97. Are Windows Defender Security Center changes recognized early enough to be approved through the regular process?
<--- Score

98. Which Windows Defender Security Center data should be retained?
<--- Score

99. Is there a strict change management process?
<--- Score

100. Did any additional data need to be collected?
<--- Score

101. What Windows Defender Security Center data should be managed?
<--- Score

102. How do your work systems and key work processes relate to and capitalize on your core competencies?
<--- Score

103. Did any value-added analysis or 'lean thinking' take place to identify some of the gaps shown on the 'as is' process map?
<--- Score

104. Do you understand your management processes today?
<--- Score

105. Is the performance gap determined?
<--- Score

106. What successful thing are you doing today that may be blinding you to new growth opportunities?
<--- Score

107. What did the team gain from developing a sub-process map?
<--- Score

108. Who is involved with workflow mapping?
<--- Score

109. What are the best opportunities for value improvement?
<--- Score

110. How is the data gathered?
<--- Score

111. How are outputs preserved and protected?
<--- Score

112. Who will facilitate the team and process?
<--- Score

113. What conclusions were drawn from the team's data collection and analysis? How did the team reach these conclusions?
<--- Score

114. What methods do you use to gather Windows Defender Security Center data?
<--- Score

115. Who qualifies to gain access to data?
<--- Score

116. Were any designed experiments used to generate additional insight into the data analysis?
<--- Score

117. Where can you get qualified talent today?
<--- Score

118. What systems/processes must you excel at?
<--- Score

119. A compounding model resolution with available relevant data can often provide insight towards a solution methodology; which Windows Defender Security Center models, tools and techniques are necessary?

<--- Score

120. Were there any improvement opportunities identified from the process analysis?
<--- Score

121. How was the detailed process map generated, verified, and validated?
<--- Score

122. How many input/output points does it require?
<--- Score

123. What Windows Defender Security Center data should be collected?
<--- Score

124. What types of data do your Windows Defender Security Center indicators require?
<--- Score

125. What were the financial benefits resulting from any 'ground fruit or low-hanging fruit' (quick fixes)?
<--- Score

126. What is your organizations system for selecting qualified vendors?
<--- Score

127. Who gets your output?
<--- Score

128. Have the problem and goal statements been updated to reflect the additional knowledge gained from the analyze phase?
<--- Score

129. How will the change process be managed?
<--- Score

130. What will drive Windows Defender Security Center change?
<--- Score

131. What are your best practices for minimizing Windows Defender Security Center project risk, while demonstrating incremental value and quick wins throughout the Windows Defender Security Center project lifecycle?
<--- Score

Add up total points for this section:
_____ = Total points for this section

Divided by: _____ (number of statements answered) = _____
Average score for this section

Transfer your score to the Windows Defender Security Center Index at the beginning of the Self-Assessment.

CRITERION #5: IMPROVE:

INTENT: Develop a practical solution. Innovate, establish and test the solution and to measure the results.

In my belief, the answer to this question is clearly defined:

5 Strongly Agree

4 Agree

3 Neutral

2 Disagree

1 Strongly Disagree

1. Who should make the Windows Defender Security Center decisions?
<--- Score

2. How do the Windows Defender Security Center results compare with the performance of your competitors and other organizations with similar offerings?
<--- Score

3. Who controls key decisions that will be made?
<--- Score

4. What can you do to improve?
<--- Score

5. What do you want to improve?
<--- Score

6. What is the risk?
<--- Score

7. What does the 'should be' process map/design look like?
<--- Score

8. What Windows Defender Security Center improvements can be made?
<--- Score

9. What error proofing will be done to address some of the discrepancies observed in the 'as is' process?
<--- Score

10. How do you measure progress and evaluate training effectiveness?
<--- Score

11. How do you manage Windows Defender Security Center risk?
<--- Score

12. What tools were used to tap into the creativity and encourage 'outside the box' thinking?
<--- Score

13. What is the magnitude of the improvements?
<--- Score

14. How do you improve your likelihood of success ?
<--- Score

15. Who are the Windows Defender Security Center decision makers?
<--- Score

16. Do you combine technical expertise with business knowledge and Windows Defender Security Center Key topics include lifecycles, development approaches, requirements and how to make a business case?
<--- Score

17. How will you know when its improved?
<--- Score

18. What alternative responses are available to manage risk?
<--- Score

19. What risks do you need to manage?
<--- Score

20. Is the Windows Defender Security Center documentation thorough?
<--- Score

21. How will you recognize and celebrate results?
<--- Score

22. Have you achieved Windows Defender Security

Center improvements?
<--- Score

23. Are events managed to resolution?
<--- Score

24. When you map the key players in your own work and the types/domains of relationships with them, which relationships do you find easy and which challenging, and why?
<--- Score

25. Do those selected for the Windows Defender Security Center team have a good general understanding of what Windows Defender Security Center is all about?
<--- Score

26. What practices helps your organization to develop its capacity to recognize patterns?
<--- Score

27. Is the solution technically practical?
<--- Score

28. How significant is the improvement in the eyes of the end user?
<--- Score

29. For estimation problems, how do you develop an estimation statement?
<--- Score

30. Who makes the Windows Defender Security Center decisions in your organization?
<--- Score

31. Why improve in the first place?
<--- Score

32. If you could go back in time five years, what decision would you make differently? What is your best guess as to what decision you're making today you might regret five years from now?
<--- Score

33. Who are the key stakeholders for the Windows Defender Security Center evaluation?
<--- Score

34. Who are the Windows Defender Security Center decision-makers?
<--- Score

35. How do you define the solutions' scope?
<--- Score

36. Is the scope clearly documented?
<--- Score

37. Will the controls trigger any other risks?
<--- Score

38. Is the measure of success for Windows Defender Security Center understandable to a variety of people?
<--- Score

39. How are policy decisions made and where?
<--- Score

40. How will you measure the results?

<--- Score

41. Risk events: what are the things that could go wrong?

<--- Score

42. What criteria will you use to assess your Windows Defender Security Center risks?

<--- Score

43. How does the team improve its work?

<--- Score

44. Do vendor agreements bring new compliance risk ?

<--- Score

45. Who controls the risk?

<--- Score

46. Are the most efficient solutions problem-specific?

<--- Score

47. Explorations of the frontiers of Windows Defender Security Center will help you build influence, improve Windows Defender Security Center, optimize decision making, and sustain change, what is your approach?

<--- Score

48. Risk factors: what are the characteristics of Windows Defender Security Center that make it risky?

<--- Score

49. Which of the recognised risks out of all risks can be most likely transferred?

<--- Score

50. How do you manage and improve your Windows Defender Security Center work systems to deliver customer value and achieve organizational success and sustainability?
<--- Score

51. What is the team's contingency plan for potential problems occurring in implementation?
<--- Score

52. How is knowledge sharing about risk management improved?
<--- Score

53. Who will be responsible for making the decisions to include or exclude requested changes once Windows Defender Security Center is underway?
<--- Score

54. What are your current levels and trends in key measures or indicators of workforce and leader development?
<--- Score

55. Does a good decision guarantee a good outcome?
<--- Score

56. Is the Windows Defender Security Center solution sustainable?
<--- Score

57. Are you assessing Windows Defender Security Center and risk?
<--- Score

58. Can you identify any significant risks or exposures to Windows Defender Security Center third- parties (vendors, service providers, alliance partners etc) that concern you?
<--- Score

59. What are the concrete Windows Defender Security Center results?
<--- Score

60. How do you go about comparing Windows Defender Security Center approaches/solutions?
<--- Score

61. Are risk triggers captured?
<--- Score

62. Who do you report Windows Defender Security Center results to?
<--- Score

63. What are the expected Windows Defender Security Center results?
<--- Score

64. How will you know that you have improved?
<--- Score

65. What actually has to improve and by how much?
<--- Score

66. Is risk periodically assessed?
<--- Score

67. Who do you report Windows Defender Security

Center results to?
<--- Score

68. What is the Windows Defender Security Center's sustainability risk?
<--- Score

69. How scalable is your Windows Defender Security Center solution?
<--- Score

70. What are the implications of the one critical Windows Defender Security Center decision 10 minutes, 10 months, and 10 years from now?
<--- Score

71. Do you cover the five essential competencies: Communication, Collaboration, Innovation, Adaptability, and Leadership that improve an organizations ability to leverage the new Windows Defender Security Center in a volatile global economy?
<--- Score

72. Windows Defender Security Center risk decisions: whose call Is It?
<--- Score

73. At what point will vulnerability assessments be performed once Windows Defender Security Center is put into production (e.g., ongoing Risk Management after implementation)?
<--- Score

74. Who are the people involved in developing and implementing Windows Defender Security Center?

<--- Score

75. Do you need to do a usability evaluation?
<--- Score

76. What were the criteria for evaluating a Windows Defender Security Center pilot?
<--- Score

77. What went well, what should change, what can improve?
<--- Score

78. Risk Identification: What are the possible risk events your organization faces in relation to Windows Defender Security Center?
<--- Score

79. Where do the Windows Defender Security Center decisions reside?
<--- Score

80. How risky is your organization?
<--- Score

81. Was a pilot designed for the proposed solution(s)?
<--- Score

82. How do you mitigate Windows Defender Security Center risk?
<--- Score

83. Does the goal represent a desired result that can be measured?
<--- Score

84. Which Windows Defender Security Center solution is appropriate?
<--- Score

85. Are decisions made in a timely manner?
<--- Score

86. What to do with the results or outcomes of measurements?
<--- Score

87. What communications are necessary to support the implementation of the solution?
<--- Score

88. What needs improvement? Why?
<--- Score

89. Who manages supplier risk management in your organization?
<--- Score

90. What tools were used to evaluate the potential solutions?
<--- Score

91. How can you better manage risk?
<--- Score

92. How can you improve performance?
<--- Score

93. Who will be using the results of the measurement activities?
<--- Score

94. How can you improve Windows Defender Security Center?

<--- Score

95. Are the key business and technology risks being managed?

<--- Score

96. Is any Windows Defender Security Center documentation required?

<--- Score

97. What lessons, if any, from a pilot were incorporated into the design of the full-scale solution?

<--- Score

98. How do you measure improved Windows Defender Security Center service perception, and satisfaction?

<--- Score

99. How will you know that a change is an improvement?

<--- Score

100. Would you develop a Windows Defender Security Center Communication Strategy?

<--- Score

101. What is Windows Defender Security Center's impact on utilizing the best solution(s)?

<--- Score

102. Are risk management tasks balanced centrally and locally?

<--- Score

103. What should a proof of concept or pilot accomplish?
<--- Score

104. What is the implementation plan?
<--- Score

105. What were the underlying assumptions on the cost-benefit analysis?
<--- Score

106. What resources are required for the improvement efforts?
<--- Score

107. How do you deal with Windows Defender Security Center risk?
<--- Score

108. Are procedures documented for managing Windows Defender Security Center risks?
<--- Score

109. How do you improve Windows Defender Security Center service perception, and satisfaction?
<--- Score

110. What is Windows Defender Security Center risk?
<--- Score

111. Where do you need Windows Defender Security Center improvement?
<--- Score

112. Have you identified breakpoints and/or risk

tolerances that will trigger broad consideration of a potential need for intervention or modification of strategy?
<--- Score

113. How does your organization evaluate strategic Windows Defender Security Center success?
<--- Score

114. To what extent does management recognize Windows Defender Security Center as a tool to increase the results?
<--- Score

115. What strategies for Windows Defender Security Center improvement are successful?
<--- Score

116. Who manages Windows Defender Security Center risk?
<--- Score

117. Were any criteria developed to assist the team in testing and evaluating potential solutions?
<--- Score

118. How do you measure risk?
<--- Score

119. Is there any other Windows Defender Security Center solution?
<--- Score

120. Who will be responsible for documenting the Windows Defender Security Center requirements in detail?

<--- Score

121. What tools were most useful during the improve phase?
<--- Score

122. What are the Windows Defender Security Center security risks?
<--- Score

123. How can skill-level changes improve Windows Defender Security Center?
<--- Score

124. What attendant changes will need to be made to ensure that the solution is successful?
<--- Score

125. Can the solution be designed and implemented within an acceptable time period?
<--- Score

126. Is the Windows Defender Security Center risk managed?
<--- Score

127. How do you link measurement and risk?
<--- Score

128. How do you keep improving Windows Defender Security Center?
<--- Score

129. Can you integrate quality management and risk management?
<--- Score

130. How do you improve productivity?
<--- Score

Add up total points for this section:
_____ = Total points for this section

Divided by: _____ (number of statements answered) = _____
Average score for this section

Transfer your score to the Windows Defender Security Center Index at the beginning of the Self-Assessment.

CRITERION #6: CONTROL:

INTENT: Implement the practical solution. Maintain the performance and correct possible complications.

In my belief, the answer to this question is clearly defined:

5 Strongly Agree

4 Agree

3 Neutral

2 Disagree

1 Strongly Disagree

1. What Windows Defender Security Center standards are applicable?
<--- Score

2. What are you attempting to measure/monitor?
<--- Score

3. Do you monitor the effectiveness of your Windows Defender Security Center activities?

<--- Score

4. Are controls in place and consistently applied?
<--- Score

5. Are the Windows Defender Security Center standards challenging?
<--- Score

6. Is a response plan in place for when the input, process, or output measures indicate an 'out-of-control' condition?
<--- Score

7. How do you spread information?
<--- Score

8. Has the Windows Defender Security Center value of standards been quantified?
<--- Score

9. What should you measure to verify efficiency gains?
<--- Score

10. What is the control/monitoring plan?
<--- Score

11. Has the improved process and its steps been standardized?
<--- Score

12. What quality tools were useful in the control phase?
<--- Score

13. Can you adapt and adjust to changing Windows

Defender Security Center situations?
<--- Score

14. How do you plan for the cost of succession?
<--- Score

15. What other areas of the group might benefit from the Windows Defender Security Center team's improvements, knowledge, and learning?
<--- Score

16. You may have created your quality measures at a time when you lacked resources, technology wasn't up to the required standard, or low service levels were the industry norm. Have those circumstances changed?
<--- Score

17. How will input, process, and output variables be checked to detect for sub-optimal conditions?
<--- Score

18. How can you best use all of your knowledge repositories to enhance learning and sharing?
<--- Score

19. Is there documentation that will support the successful operation of the improvement?
<--- Score

20. What can you control?
<--- Score

21. How do your controls stack up?
<--- Score

22. Is a response plan established and deployed?
<--- Score

23. Do the viable solutions scale to future needs?
<--- Score

24. Who controls critical resources?
<--- Score

25. How might the group capture best practices and lessons learned so as to leverage improvements?
<--- Score

26. What are your results for key measures or indicators of the accomplishment of your Windows Defender Security Center strategy and action plans, including building and strengthening core competencies?
<--- Score

27. Will any special training be provided for results interpretation?
<--- Score

28. How do controls support value?
<--- Score

29. What key inputs and outputs are being measured on an ongoing basis?
<--- Score

30. How will you measure your QA plan's effectiveness?
<--- Score

31. How will the process owner and team be able to

hold the gains?
<--- Score

32. In the case of a Windows Defender Security Center project, the criteria for the audit derive from implementation objectives, an audit of a Windows Defender Security Center project involves assessing whether the recommendations outlined for implementation have been met, can you track that any Windows Defender Security Center project is implemented as planned, and is it working?
<--- Score

33. What do you stand for--and what are you against?
<--- Score

34. How do you monitor usage and cost?
<--- Score

35. How will Windows Defender Security Center decisions be made and monitored?
<--- Score

36. Will your goals reflect your program budget?
<--- Score

37. Is there a recommended audit plan for routine surveillance inspections of Windows Defender Security Center's gains?
<--- Score

38. Do the Windows Defender Security Center decisions you make today help people and the planet tomorrow?
<--- Score

39. Is there an action plan in case of emergencies?
<--- Score

40. Are documented procedures clear and easy to follow for the operators?
<--- Score

41. Does job training on the documented procedures need to be part of the process team's education and training?
<--- Score

42. What are the critical parameters to watch?
<--- Score

43. Is there a control plan in place for sustaining improvements (short and long-term)?
<--- Score

44. Are operating procedures consistent?
<--- Score

45. What is the recommended frequency of auditing?
<--- Score

46. How is Windows Defender Security Center project cost planned, managed, monitored?
<--- Score

47. Is there a standardized process?
<--- Score

48. What should the next improvement project be that is related to Windows Defender Security Center?
<--- Score

49. Is there a transfer of ownership and knowledge to process owner and process team tasked with the responsibilities.

<--- Score

50. What are the known security controls?

<--- Score

51. How will new or emerging customer needs/requirements be checked/communicated to orient the process toward meeting the new specifications and continually reducing variation?

<--- Score

52. Is reporting being used or needed?

<--- Score

53. Have new or revised work instructions resulted?

<--- Score

54. What is your plan to assess your security risks?

<--- Score

55. Where do ideas that reach policy makers and planners as proposals for Windows Defender Security Center strengthening and reform actually originate?

<--- Score

56. How will the day-to-day responsibilities for monitoring and continual improvement be transferred from the improvement team to the process owner?

<--- Score

57. Are there documented procedures?

<--- Score

58. How do you select, collect, align, and integrate Windows Defender Security Center data and information for tracking daily operations and overall organizational performance, including progress relative to strategic objectives and action plans?
<--- Score

59. Does Windows Defender Security Center appropriately measure and monitor risk?
<--- Score

60. Is there a Windows Defender Security Center Communication plan covering who needs to get what information when?
<--- Score

61. What do your reports reflect?
<--- Score

62. Will the team be available to assist members in planning investigations?
<--- Score

63. How will report readings be checked to effectively monitor performance?
<--- Score

64. Who is going to spread your message?
<--- Score

65. Are the planned controls in place?
<--- Score

66. What other systems, operations, processes, and infrastructures (hiring practices, staffing, training,

incentives/rewards, metrics/dashboards/scorecards, etc.) need updates, additions, changes, or deletions in order to facilitate knowledge transfer and improvements?
<--- Score

67. Does a troubleshooting guide exist or is it needed?
<--- Score

68. Does the response plan contain a definite closed loop continual improvement scheme (e.g., plan-do-check-act)?
<--- Score

69. Who sets the Windows Defender Security Center standards?
<--- Score

70. How will the process owner verify improvement in present and future sigma levels, process capabilities?
<--- Score

71. What adjustments to the strategies are needed?
<--- Score

72. What is the best design framework for Windows Defender Security Center organization now that, in a post industrial-age if the top-down, command and control model is no longer relevant?
<--- Score

73. What are the key elements of your Windows Defender Security Center performance improvement system, including your evaluation, organizational learning, and innovation processes?
<--- Score

74. What are the performance and scale of the Windows Defender Security Center tools?
<--- Score

75. Is knowledge gained on process shared and institutionalized?
<--- Score

76. Is there a documented and implemented monitoring plan?
<--- Score

77. What is your theory of human motivation, and how does your compensation plan fit with that view?
<--- Score

78. How likely is the current Windows Defender Security Center plan to come in on schedule or on budget?
<--- Score

79. Are pertinent alerts monitored, analyzed and distributed to appropriate personnel?
<--- Score

80. What is the standard for acceptable Windows Defender Security Center performance?
<--- Score

81. Do you monitor the Windows Defender Security Center decisions made and fine tune them as they evolve?
<--- Score

82. How is change control managed?

<--- Score

83. Is the Windows Defender Security Center test/monitoring cost justified?
<--- Score

84. How do you plan on providing proper recognition and disclosure of supporting companies?
<--- Score

85. Are suggested corrective/restorative actions indicated on the response plan for known causes to problems that might surface?
<--- Score

86. How do you establish and deploy modified action plans if circumstances require a shift in plans and rapid execution of new plans?
<--- Score

87. Are the planned controls working?
<--- Score

88. Implementation Planning: is a pilot needed to test the changes before a full roll out occurs?
<--- Score

89. What are customers monitoring?
<--- Score

90. Will existing staff require re-training, for example, to learn new business processes?
<--- Score

91. Who will be in control?

<--- Score

92. Can support from partners be adjusted?
<--- Score

93. Are new process steps, standards, and documentation ingrained into normal operations?
<--- Score

94. How do you encourage people to take control and responsibility?
<--- Score

95. Are you measuring, monitoring and predicting Windows Defender Security Center activities to optimize operations and profitability, and enhancing outcomes?
<--- Score

96. Does the Windows Defender Security Center performance meet the customer's requirements?
<--- Score

97. Is new knowledge gained imbedded in the response plan?
<--- Score

98. Who is the Windows Defender Security Center process owner?
<--- Score

99. Against what alternative is success being measured?
<--- Score

Add up total points for this section:

_____ = Total points for this section

Divided by: _____ (number of statements answered) = _____
Average score for this section

Transfer your score to the Windows Defender Security Center Index at the beginning of the Self-Assessment.

CRITERION #7: SUSTAIN:

INTENT: Retain the benefits.

In my belief, the answer to this question is clearly defined:

5 Strongly Agree

4 Agree

3 Neutral

2 Disagree

1 Strongly Disagree

1. Who are your customers?
<--- Score

2. Is your strategy driving your strategy? Or is the way in which you allocate resources driving your strategy?
<--- Score

3. If your customer were your grandmother, would you tell her to buy what you're selling?
<--- Score

4. What Windows Defender Security Center skills are most important?
<--- Score

5. What are strategies for increasing support and reducing opposition?
<--- Score

6. What are the gaps in your knowledge and experience?
<--- Score

7. Where can you break convention?
<--- Score

8. Are you / should you be revolutionary or evolutionary?
<--- Score

9. How do you know if you are successful?
<--- Score

10. How do you foster the skills, knowledge, talents, attributes, and characteristics you want to have?
<--- Score

11. If you had to rebuild your organization without any traditional competitive advantages (i.e., no killer technology, promising research, innovative product/service delivery model, etcetera), how would your people have to approach their work and collaborate together in order to create the necessary conditions for success?
<--- Score

12. Do you have past Windows Defender Security

Center successes?
<--- Score

13. Did your employees make progress today?
<--- Score

14. What are your personal philosophies regarding Windows Defender Security Center and how do they influence your work?
<--- Score

15. How do you track customer value, profitability or financial return, organizational success, and sustainability?
<--- Score

16. What are internal and external Windows Defender Security Center relations?
<--- Score

17. How can you incorporate support to ensure safe and effective use of Windows Defender Security Center into the services that you provide?
<--- Score

18. Who, on the executive team or the board, has spoken to a customer recently?
<--- Score

19. What is the funding source for this project?
<--- Score

20. What is your competitive advantage?
<--- Score

21. Is it economical; do you have the time and money?

<--- Score

22. Why will customers want to buy your organizations products/services?
<--- Score

23. How do you engage the workforce, in addition to satisfying them?
<--- Score

24. Ask yourself: how would you do this work if you only had one staff member to do it?
<--- Score

25. Why should people listen to you?
<--- Score

26. Who is the main stakeholder, with ultimate responsibility for driving Windows Defender Security Center forward?
<--- Score

27. What are the key enablers to make this Windows Defender Security Center move?
<--- Score

28. How can you become the company that would put you out of business?
<--- Score

29. What are specific Windows Defender Security Center rules to follow?
<--- Score

30. Is your basic point _____ or _____?
<--- Score

31. What you are going to do to affect the numbers?
<--- Score

32. What are you trying to prove to yourself, and how might it be hijacking your life and business success?
<--- Score

33. What are current Windows Defender Security Center paradigms?
<--- Score

34. Can the schedule be done in the given time?
<--- Score

35. What is the estimated value of the project?
<--- Score

36. How do you go about securing Windows Defender Security Center?
<--- Score

37. What are the potential basics of Windows Defender Security Center fraud?
<--- Score

38. If you got fired and a new hire took your place, what would she do different?
<--- Score

39. Who will provide the final approval of Windows Defender Security Center deliverables?
<--- Score

40. How do you determine the key elements that affect Windows Defender Security Center

workforce satisfaction, how are these elements determined for different workforce groups and segments?

<--- Score

41. How do you govern and fulfill your societal responsibilities?

<--- Score

42. Are you paying enough attention to the partners your company depends on to succeed?

<--- Score

43. What threat is Windows Defender Security Center addressing?

<--- Score

44. Are you using a design thinking approach and integrating Innovation, Windows Defender Security Center Experience, and Brand Value?

<--- Score

45. How do you keep the momentum going?

<--- Score

46. What Windows Defender Security Center modifications can you make work for you?

<--- Score

47. Why do and why don't your customers like your organization?

<--- Score

48. What are you challenging?

<--- Score

49. How do you provide a safe environment -physically and emotionally?
<--- Score

50. How will you ensure you get what you expected?
<--- Score

51. If you had to leave your organization for a year and the only communication you could have with employees/colleagues was a single paragraph, what would you write?
<--- Score

52. How do you accomplish your long range Windows Defender Security Center goals?
<--- Score

53. Do you know what you are doing? And who do you call if you don't?
<--- Score

54. What happens if you do not have enough funding?
<--- Score

55. What is your BATNA (best alternative to a negotiated agreement)?
<--- Score

56. What is the kind of project structure that would be appropriate for your Windows Defender Security Center project, should it be formal and complex, or can it be less formal and relatively simple?
<--- Score

57. What unique value proposition (UVP) do you offer?
<--- Score

58. What is the overall business strategy?
<--- Score

59. Are you satisfied with your current role? If not, what is missing from it?
<--- Score

60. Are there any activities that you can take off your to do list?
<--- Score

61. How do you keep records, of what?
<--- Score

62. Who is responsible for Windows Defender Security Center?
<--- Score

63. How are you doing compared to your industry?
<--- Score

64. How do you create buy-in?
<--- Score

65. How will you motivate the stakeholders with the least vested interest?
<--- Score

66. Whose voice (department, ethnic group, women, older workers, etc) might you have missed hearing from in your company, and how might you amplify this voice to create positive momentum for your

business?
<--- Score

67. How do you cross-sell and up-sell your Windows Defender Security Center success?
<--- Score

68. What new services of functionality will be implemented next with Windows Defender Security Center ?
<--- Score

69. Do you know who is a friend or a foe?
<--- Score

70. Has implementation been effective in reaching specified objectives so far?
<--- Score

71. Who is responsible for errors?
<--- Score

72. Have new benefits been realized?
<--- Score

73. How much does Windows Defender Security Center help?
<--- Score

74. What does your signature ensure?
<--- Score

75. Who do we want your customers to become?
<--- Score

76. Marketing budgets are tighter, consumers are

more skeptical, and social media has changed forever the way we talk about Windows Defender Security Center, how do you gain traction?

<--- Score

77. What goals did you miss?

<--- Score

78. What do we do when new problems arise?

<--- Score

79. Whom among your colleagues do you trust, and for what?

<--- Score

80. What is the source of the strategies for Windows Defender Security Center strengthening and reform?

<--- Score

81. Are you relevant? Will you be relevant five years from now? Ten?

<--- Score

82. How do you listen to customers to obtain actionable information?

<--- Score

83. How do you deal with Windows Defender Security Center changes?

<--- Score

84. Do you say no to customers for no reason?

<--- Score

85. Is there a work around that you can use?

<--- Score

86. How do customers see your organization?
<--- Score

87. What business benefits will Windows Defender Security Center goals deliver if achieved?
<--- Score

88. Who are four people whose careers you have enhanced?
<--- Score

89. What was the last experiment you ran?
<--- Score

90. What is your formula for success in Windows Defender Security Center ?
<--- Score

91. How do you foster innovation?
<--- Score

92. How do you proactively clarify deliverables and Windows Defender Security Center quality expectations?
<--- Score

93. What must you excel at?
<--- Score

94. If you find that you havent accomplished one of the goals for one of the steps of the Windows Defender Security Center strategy, what will you do to fix it?
<--- Score

95. Who are the key stakeholders?
<--- Score

96. Who is on the team?
<--- Score

97. What are the challenges?
<--- Score

98. Who do you think the world wants your organization to be?
<--- Score

99. Are the assumptions believable and achievable?
<--- Score

100. What would you recommend your friend do if he/she were facing this dilemma?
<--- Score

101. Are you changing as fast as the world around you?
<--- Score

102. What information is critical to your organization that your executives are ignoring?
<--- Score

103. Is the Windows Defender Security Center organization completing tasks effectively and efficiently?
<--- Score

104. Which models, tools and techniques are necessary?
<--- Score

105. What are the top 3 things at the forefront of your Windows Defender Security Center agendas for the next 3 years?
<--- Score

106. What is your question? Why?
<--- Score

107. Instead of going to current contacts for new ideas, what if you reconnected with dormant contacts--the people you used to know? If you were going reactivate a dormant tie, who would it be?
<--- Score

108. What trophy do you want on your mantle?
<--- Score

109. How do senior leaders deploy your organizations vision and values through your leadership system, to the workforce, to key suppliers and partners, and to customers and other stakeholders, as appropriate?
<--- Score

110. If you weren't already in this business, would you enter it today? And if not, what are you going to do about it?
<--- Score

111. What are the long-term Windows Defender Security Center goals?
<--- Score

112. Are your responses positive or negative?
<--- Score

113. How important is Windows Defender Security Center to the user organizations mission?
<--- Score

114. Do you think you know, or do you know you know ?
<--- Score

115. What relationships among Windows Defender Security Center trends do you perceive?
<--- Score

116. Would you rather sell to knowledgeable and informed customers or to uninformed customers?
<--- Score

117. Have benefits been optimized with all key stakeholders?
<--- Score

118. What is a feasible sequencing of reform initiatives over time?
<--- Score

119. What did you miss in the interview for the worst hire you ever made?
<--- Score

120. In the past year, what have you done (or could you have done) to increase the accurate perception of your company/brand as ethical and honest?
<--- Score

121. Who will manage the integration of tools?
<--- Score

122. What are the business goals Windows Defender Security Center is aiming to achieve?
<--- Score

123. Are new benefits received and understood?
<--- Score

124. How do you set Windows Defender Security Center stretch targets and how do you get people to not only participate in setting these stretch targets but also that they strive to achieve these?
<--- Score

125. Why is Windows Defender Security Center important for you now?
<--- Score

126. What are the success criteria that will indicate that Windows Defender Security Center objectives have been met and the benefits delivered?
<--- Score

127. Why not do Windows Defender Security Center?
<--- Score

128. At what moment would you think; Will I get fired?
<--- Score

129. How will you know that the Windows Defender Security Center project has been successful?
<--- Score

130. Can you maintain your growth without

detracting from the factors that have contributed to your success?
<--- Score

131. Are all key stakeholders present at all Structured Walkthroughs?
<--- Score

132. What have you done to protect your business from competitive encroachment?
<--- Score

133. Who will determine interim and final deadlines?
<--- Score

134. Is Windows Defender Security Center realistic, or are you setting yourself up for failure?
<--- Score

135. What happens at your organization when people fail?
<--- Score

136. What knowledge, skills and characteristics mark a good Windows Defender Security Center project manager?
<--- Score

137. What is the craziest thing you can do?
<--- Score

138. What is the recommended frequency of auditing?
<--- Score

139. What should you stop doing?

<--- Score

140. Is there any existing Windows Defender Security Center governance structure?

<--- Score

141. In retrospect, of the projects that you pulled the plug on, what percent do you wish had been allowed to keep going, and what percent do you wish had ended earlier?

<--- Score

142. What current systems have to be understood and/or changed?

<--- Score

143. How do you assess the Windows Defender Security Center pitfalls that are inherent in implementing it?

<--- Score

144. What is your Windows Defender Security Center strategy?

<--- Score

145. What projects are going on in the organization today, and what resources are those projects using from the resource pools?

<--- Score

146. How much contingency will be available in the budget?

<--- Score

147. Do you have enough freaky customers in your

portfolio pushing you to the limit day in and day out?
<--- Score

148. Political -is anyone trying to undermine this project?
<--- Score

149. If you do not follow, then how to lead?
<--- Score

150. What is something you believe that nearly no one agrees with you on?
<--- Score

151. What are your most important goals for the strategic Windows Defender Security Center objectives?
<--- Score

152. Which Windows Defender Security Center goals are the most important?
<--- Score

153. What are the rules and assumptions your industry operates under? What if the opposite were true?
<--- Score

154. How is implementation research currently incorporated into each of your goals?
<--- Score

155. To whom do you add value?
<--- Score

156. What will be the consequences to the stakeholder (financial, reputation etc) if Windows

Defender Security Center does not go ahead or fails to deliver the objectives?
<--- Score

157. What trouble can you get into?
<--- Score

158. How do you ensure that implementations of Windows Defender Security Center products are done in a way that ensures safety?
<--- Score

159. In a project to restructure Windows Defender Security Center outcomes, which stakeholders would you involve?
<--- Score

160. Are assumptions made in Windows Defender Security Center stated explicitly?
<--- Score

161. What role does communication play in the success or failure of a Windows Defender Security Center project?
<--- Score

162. Will there be any necessary staff changes (redundancies or new hires)?
<--- Score

163. How do you stay inspired?
<--- Score

164. If you were responsible for initiating and implementing major changes in your organization, what steps might you take to ensure acceptance of

those changes?
<--- Score

165. How likely is it that a customer would recommend your company to a friend or colleague?
<--- Score

166. Do Windows Defender Security Center rules make a reasonable demand on a users capabilities?
<--- Score

167. Were lessons learned captured and communicated?
<--- Score

168. Who uses your product in ways you never expected?
<--- Score

169. If no one would ever find out about your accomplishments, how would you lead differently?
<--- Score

170. What one word do you want to own in the minds of your customers, employees, and partners?
<--- Score

171. Which functions and people interact with the supplier and or customer?
<--- Score

172. What is the purpose of Windows Defender Security Center in relation to the mission?
<--- Score

173. How do you manage Windows Defender Security Center Knowledge Management (KM)?

<--- Score

174. Operational - will it work?

<--- Score

175. What are the barriers to increased Windows Defender Security Center production?

<--- Score

176. What is the overall talent health of your organization as a whole at senior levels, and for each organization reporting to a member of the Senior Leadership Team?

<--- Score

177. Who have you, as a company, historically been when you've been at your best?

<--- Score

178. If your company went out of business tomorrow, would anyone who doesn't get a paycheck here care?

<--- Score

179. What would have to be true for the option on the table to be the best possible choice?

<--- Score

180. Can you do all this work?

<--- Score

181. Who else should you help?

<--- Score

182. What is the range of capabilities?
<--- Score

183. What counts that you are not counting?
<--- Score

184. How do you decide how much to remunerate an employee?
<--- Score

185. Is a Windows Defender Security Center breakthrough on the horizon?
<--- Score

186. What is it like to work for you?
<--- Score

187. How do you lead with Windows Defender Security Center in mind?
<--- Score

188. Who will be responsible for deciding whether Windows Defender Security Center goes ahead or not after the initial investigations?
<--- Score

189. What stupid rule would you most like to kill?
<--- Score

190. Is maximizing Windows Defender Security Center protection the same as minimizing Windows Defender Security Center loss?
<--- Score

191. Why should you adopt a Windows Defender Security Center framework?

<--- Score

192. Who do you want your customers to become?
<--- Score

193. Is there any reason to believe the opposite of my current belief?
<--- Score

194. Is the impact that Windows Defender Security Center has shown?
<--- Score

195. If there were zero limitations, what would you do differently?
<--- Score

196. Do you see more potential in people than they do in themselves?
<--- Score

197. Do you have an implicit bias for capital investments over people investments?
<--- Score

198. Do you have the right capabilities and capacities?
<--- Score

199. Think of your Windows Defender Security Center project, what are the main functions?
<--- Score

200. Do you think Windows Defender Security Center accomplishes the goals you expect it to accomplish?

<--- Score

201. What is effective Windows Defender Security Center?
<--- Score

202. What may be the consequences for the performance of an organization if all stakeholders are not consulted regarding Windows Defender Security Center?
<--- Score

203. How can you become more high-tech but still be high touch?
<--- Score

204. How do you maintain Windows Defender Security Center's Integrity?
<--- Score

205. Is a Windows Defender Security Center team work effort in place?
<--- Score

206. Are you maintaining a past–present–future perspective throughout the Windows Defender Security Center discussion?
<--- Score

207. Do you have the right people on the bus?
<--- Score

208. When information truly is ubiquitous, when reach and connectivity are completely global, when computing resources are infinite, and when a whole new set of impossibilities are not only possible, but

happening, what will that do to your business?
<--- Score

209. Will it be accepted by users?
<--- Score

210. Which individuals, teams or departments will be involved in Windows Defender Security Center?
<--- Score

211. How long will it take to change?
<--- Score

212. How do you make it meaningful in connecting Windows Defender Security Center with what users do day-to-day?
<--- Score

213. How does Windows Defender Security Center integrate with other stakeholder initiatives?
<--- Score

214. What have been your experiences in defining long range Windows Defender Security Center goals?
<--- Score

215. Are you making progress, and are you making progress as Windows Defender Security Center leaders?
<--- Score

216. What management system can you use to leverage the Windows Defender Security Center experience, ideas, and concerns of the people closest to the work to be done?

<--- Score

Add up total points for this section:
_____ = Total points for this section

Divided by: _____ (number of statements answered) = _____
Average score for this section

Transfer your score to the Windows Defender Security Center Index at the beginning of the Self-Assessment.

Windows Defender Security Center and Managing Projects, Criteria for Project Managers:

1.0 Initiating Process Group: Windows Defender Security Center

1. Who supports, improves, and oversees standardized processes related to the Windows Defender Security Center projects program?

2. Contingency planning. if a risk event occurs, what will you do?

3. How will you know you did it?

4. When are the deliverables to be generated in each phase?

5. Specific - is the objective clear in terms of what, how, when, and where the situation will be changed?

6. Who is funding the Windows Defender Security Center project?

7. Have the stakeholders identified all individual requirements pertaining to business process?

8. Do you know if the Windows Defender Security Center project requires outside equipment or vendor resources?

9. What were the challenges that you encountered during the execution of a previous Windows Defender Security Center project that you would not want to repeat?

10. What technical work to do in each phase?

11. Did the Windows Defender Security Center project team have the right skills?

12. Were resources available as planned?

13. How well did the chosen processes fit the needs of the Windows Defender Security Center project?

14. Measurable - are the targets measurable?

15. At which cmmi level are software processes documented, standardized, and integrated into a standard to-be practiced process for your organization?

16. Have you evaluated the teams performance and asked for feedback?

17. How is each deliverable reviewed, verified, and validated?

18. Do you know the roles & responsibilities required for this Windows Defender Security Center project?

19. What are the required resources?

20. Are identified risks being monitored properly, are new risks arising during the Windows Defender Security Center project or are foreseen risks occurring?

1.1 Project Charter: Windows Defender Security Center

21. What is the justification?

22. Who are the stakeholders?

23. Windows Defender Security Center project background: what is the primary motivation for this Windows Defender Security Center project?

24. Who is the Windows Defender Security Center project Manager?

25. When is a charter needed?

26. Run it as as a startup?

27. What are some examples of a business case?

28. Must Have?

29. When do you use a Windows Defender Security Center project Charter?

30. When will this occur?

31. Windows Defender Security Center project objective statement: what must the Windows Defender Security Center project do?

32. What material?

33. Windows Defender Security Center project deliverables: what is the Windows Defender Security Center project going to produce?

34. Why Outsource?

35. Is it an improvement over existing products?

36. Why use a Windows Defender Security Center project charter?

37. How will you know that a change is an improvement?

38. Fit with other Products Compliments – Cannibalizes?

39. What are the known stakeholder requirements?

40. Why do you need to manage scope?

1.2 Stakeholder Register: Windows Defender Security Center

41. How much influence do they have on the Windows Defender Security Center project?

42. How should employers make voices heard?

43. What & Why?

44. Who wants to talk about Security?

45. How big is the gap?

46. How will reports be created?

47. What are the major Windows Defender Security Center project milestones requiring communications or providing communications opportunities?

48. What opportunities exist to provide communications?

49. What is the power of the stakeholder?

50. Is your organization ready for change?

51. Who is managing stakeholder engagement?

1.3 Stakeholder Analysis Matrix: Windows Defender Security Center

52. How do you manage Windows Defender Security Center project Risk?

53. How to measure the achievement of the Development Objective?

54. Who will be responsible for managing the outcome?

55. Identify the stakeholders levels most frequently used –or at least sought– in your Windows Defender Security Center projects and for which purpose?

56. Guiding question: what is the issue at stake?

57. How will the stakeholder directly benefit from the Windows Defender Security Center project and how will this affect the stakeholders motivation?

58. Vital contracts and partners?

59. Geographical, export, import?

60. What unique or lowest-cost resources does the Windows Defender Security Center project have access to?

61. How does the Windows Defender Security Center project involve consultations or collaboration with other organizations?

62. What is relationship with the Windows Defender Security Center project?

63. Inoculations or payment to receive them?

64. How can you fill the need to show progress?

65. Sustainable financial backing?

66. What do you Evaluate?

67. How to measure the achievement of the Immediate Objective?

68. How to measure the achievement of the Outputs?

69. Loss of key staff?

70. Legislative effects?

2.0 Planning Process Group: Windows Defender Security Center

71. To what extent has a PMO contributed to raising the quality of the design of the Windows Defender Security Center project?

72. If action is called for, what form should it take?

73. To what extent has the intervention strategy been adapted to the areas of intervention in which it is being implemented?

74. What do you need to do?

75. Are the necessary foundations in place to ensure the sustainability of the results of the Windows Defender Security Center project?

76. Why is it important to determine activity sequencing on Windows Defender Security Center projects?

77. What types of differentiated effects are resulting from the Windows Defender Security Center project and to what extent?

78. The Windows Defender Security Center project charter is created in which Windows Defender Security Center project management process group?

79. To what extent do the intervention objectives and strategies of the Windows Defender Security Center

project respond to your organizations plans?

80. What will you do to minimize the impact should a risk event occur?

81. If task x starts two days late, what is the effect on the Windows Defender Security Center project end date?

82. Are you just doing busywork to pass the time?

83. Will the products created live up to the necessary quality?

84. Did the program design/ implementation strategy adequately address the planning stage necessary to set up structures, hire staff etc.?

85. In what way has the program contributed towards the issue culture and development included on the public agenda?

86. Do the partners have sufficient financial capacity to keep up the benefits produced by the programme?

87. You did your readings, yes?

88. How are it Windows Defender Security Center projects different?

89. How will you do it?

90. In which Windows Defender Security Center project management process group is the detailed Windows Defender Security Center project budget created?

2.1 Project Management Plan: Windows Defender Security Center

91. What if, for example, the positive direction and vision of your organization causes expected trends to change resulting in greater need than expected?

92. What should you drop in order to add something new?

93. Development trends and opportunities. What if the positive direction and vision of your organization causes expected trends to change?

94. Is there an incremental analysis/cost effectiveness analysis of proposed mitigation features based on an approved method and using an accepted model?

95. Are cost risk analysis methods applied to develop contingencies for the estimated total Windows Defender Security Center project costs?

96. Is mitigation authorized or recommended?

97. Are there any scope changes proposed for a previously authorized Windows Defender Security Center project?

98. What are the constraints?

99. Will you add a schedule and diagram?

100. What went right?

101. How can you best help your organization to develop consistent practices in Windows Defender Security Center project management planning stages?

102. What would you do differently?

103. How do you manage time?

104. What data/reports/tools/etc. do program managers need?

105. Are there any windfall benefits that would accrue to the Windows Defender Security Center project sponsor or other parties?

106. Are there any client staffing expectations?

107. What goes into your Windows Defender Security Center project Charter?

108. Where does all this information come from?

109. Who is the Windows Defender Security Center project Manager?

2.2 Scope Management Plan: Windows Defender Security Center

110. Are enough systems & user personnel assigned to the Windows Defender Security Center project?

111. Would the Windows Defender Security Center project cost sharing involve reimbursement to the sponsor?

112. Have you identified possible roadblocks?

113. Does the Windows Defender Security Center project have a Quality Culture?

114. Are the results of quality assurance reviews provided to affected groups & individuals?

115. What threats might prevent you from getting there?

116. Has the Windows Defender Security Center project scope been baselined?

117. Has allowance been made for vacations, holidays, training (learning time for each team member), staff promotions & staff turnovers?

118. Does the Windows Defender Security Center project have a Statement of Work?

119. What happens if scope changes?

120. Was the scope definition used in task sequencing?

121. Pop quiz – which are the same inputs as in scope planning?

122. What are the risks that could significantly affect the scope of the Windows Defender Security Center project?

123. Are updated Windows Defender Security Center project time & resource estimates reasonable based on the current Windows Defender Security Center project stage?

124. Were Windows Defender Security Center project team members involved in the development of activity & task decomposition?

125. Alignment to strategic goals & objectives?

126. Has the Windows Defender Security Center project manager been identified?

127. What does the critical path really mean?

128. Is there a formal set of procedures supporting Stakeholder Management?

129. What are the risks that could significantly affect the resources needed for the Windows Defender Security Center project?

2.3 Requirements Management Plan: Windows Defender Security Center

130. Have stakeholders been instructed in the Change Control process?

131. How will you develop the schedule of requirements activities?

132. What performance metrics will be used?

133. Who is responsible for monitoring and tracking the Windows Defender Security Center project requirements?

134. The wbs is developed as part of a joint planning session. and how do you know that youhave done this right?

135. What cost metrics will be used?

136. Will you use an assessment of the Windows Defender Security Center project environment as a tool to discover risk to the requirements process?

137. Will the contractors involved take full responsibility?

138. Do you know which stakeholders will participate in the requirements effort?

139. What are you trying to do?

140. Will you have access to stakeholders when you need them?

141. Did you avoid subjective, flowery or non-specific statements?

142. Will you perform a Requirements Risk assessment and develop a plan to deal with risks?

143. After the requirements are gathered and set forth on the requirements register, theyre little more than a laundry list of items. Some may be duplicates, some might conflict with others and some will be too broad or too vague to understand. Describe how the requirements will be analyzed. Who will perform the analysis?

144. Will the Windows Defender Security Center project requirements become approved in writing?

145. Do you expect stakeholders to be cooperative?

146. Is there formal agreement on who has authority to request a change in requirements?

147. How will the requirements become prioritized?

148. Are all the stakeholders ready for the transition into the user community?

149. Who came up with this requirement?

2.4 Requirements Documentation: Windows Defender Security Center

150. What variations exist for a process?

151. Completeness. are all functions required by the customer included?

152. Validity. does the system provide the functions which best support the customers needs?

153. Basic work/business process; high-level, what is being touched?

154. Is the requirement properly understood?

155. What are the attributes of a customer?

156. How will the proposed Windows Defender Security Center project help?

157. Where are business rules being captured?

158. Who is interacting with the system?

159. What are current process problems?

160. What if the system wasn t implemented?

161. What images does it conjure?

162. How to document system requirements?

163. Can the requirement be changed without a large impact on other requirements?

164. What is effective documentation?

165. Are there legal issues?

166. What facilities must be supported by the system?

167. What is your Elevator Speech?

168. How does the proposed Windows Defender Security Center project contribute to the overall objectives of your organization?

169. Do your constraints stand?

2.5 Requirements Traceability Matrix: Windows Defender Security Center

170. Why do you manage scope?

171. What percentage of Windows Defender Security Center projects are producing traceability matrices between requirements and other work products?

172. Why use a WBS?

173. What are the chronologies, contingencies, consequences, criteria?

174. What is the WBS?

175. How do you manage scope?

176. Describe the process for approving requirements so they can be added to the traceability matrix and Windows Defender Security Center project work can be performed. Will the Windows Defender Security Center project requirements become approved in writing?

177. Is there a requirements traceability process in place?

178. How small is small enough?

179. How will it affect the stakeholders personally in career?

180. Will you use a Requirements Traceability Matrix?

181. Do you have a clear understanding of all subcontracts in place?

2.6 Project Scope Statement: Windows Defender Security Center

182. Will the Windows Defender Security Center project risks be managed according to the Windows Defender Security Center projects risk management process?

183. Have you been able to thoroughly document the Windows Defender Security Center projects assumptions and constraints?

184. What are the major deliverables of the Windows Defender Security Center project?

185. Will statistics related to QA be collected, trends analyzed, and problems raised as issues?

186. Where and how does the team fit within your organization structure?

187. Will tasks be marked complete only after QA has been successfully completed?

188. Are there completion/verification criteria defined for each task producing an output?

189. Is an issue management process documented and filed?

190. Are the meetings set up to have assigned note takers that will add action/issues to the issue list?

191. Change management vs. change leadership - what is the difference?

192. What actions will be taken to mitigate the risk?

193. Were key Windows Defender Security Center project stakeholders brought into the Windows Defender Security Center project Plan?

194. Are there issues that could affect the existing requirements for the result, service, or product if the scope changes?

195. Risks?

196. Have you been able to easily identify success criteria and create objective measurements for each of the Windows Defender Security Center project scopes goal statements?

197. Is the Windows Defender Security Center project manager qualified and experienced in Windows Defender Security Center project management?

198. How often do you estimate that the scope might change, and why?

199. Has a method and process for requirement tracking been developed?

200. Will there be a Change Control Process in place?

2.7 Assumption and Constraint Log: Windows Defender Security Center

201. Is the steering committee active in Windows Defender Security Center project oversight?

202. Are there nonconformance issues?

203. Can the requirements be traced to the appropriate components of the solution, as well as test scripts?

204. What if failure during recovery?

205. What do you audit?

206. Does the traceability documentation describe the tool and/or mechanism to be used to capture traceability throughout the life cycle?

207. Are there standards for code development?

208. Does the plan conform to standards?

209. Can you perform this task or activity in a more effective manner?

210. Have the scope, objectives, costs, benefits and impacts been communicated to all involved and/or impacted stakeholders and work groups?

211. If appropriate, is the deliverable content consistent with current Windows Defender Security

Center project documents and in compliance with the Document Management Plan?

212. What is positive about the current process?

213. Do documented requirements exist for all critical components and areas, including technical, business, interfaces, performance, security and conversion requirements?

214. Does the document/deliverable meet all requirements (for example, statement of work) specific to this deliverable?

215. Does a specific action and/or state that is known to violate security policy occur?

216. How are new requirements or changes to requirements identified?

217. What other teams / processes would be impacted by changes to the current process, and how?

218. Are there procedures in place to effectively manage interdependencies with other Windows Defender Security Center projects / systems?

219. Contradictory information between document sections?

220. What do you log?

2.8 Work Breakdown Structure: Windows Defender Security Center

221. When does it have to be done?

222. How will you and your Windows Defender Security Center project team define the Windows Defender Security Center projects scope and work breakdown structure?

223. How big is a work-package?

224. Who has to do it?

225. What is the probability that the Windows Defender Security Center project duration will exceed xx weeks?

226. Where does it take place?

227. When would you develop a Work Breakdown Structure?

228. Is it a change in scope?

229. Do you need another level?

230. Is the work breakdown structure (wbs) defined and is the scope of the Windows Defender Security Center project clear with assigned deliverable owners?

231. Is it still viable?

232. When do you stop?

233. How much detail?

234. What is the probability of completing the Windows Defender Security Center project in less that xx days?

235. Why is it useful?

236. How far down?

237. Can you make it?

2.9 WBS Dictionary: Windows Defender Security Center

238. The Windows Defender Security Center projected business base for each period?

239. Are indirect costs charged to the appropriate indirect pools and incurring organization?

240. Evaluate the performance of operating organizations?

241. Are records maintained to show how management reserves are used?

242. Contemplated overhead expenditure for each period based on the best information currently available?

243. Budgeted cost for work performed?

244. Changes in the direct base to which overhead costs are allocated?

245. What size should a work package be?

246. Budgets assigned to control accounts?

247. Are the contractors estimates of costs at completion reconcilable with cost data reported to us?

248. Are all authorized tasks assigned to identified

organizational elements?

249. Are time-phased budgets established for planning and control of level of effort activity by category of resource; for example, type of manpower and/or material?

250. Are procedures established to prevent changes to the contract budget base other than the already stated authorized by contractual action?

251. Are internal budgets for authorized, and not priced changes based on the contractors resource plan for accomplishing the work?

252. Appropriate work authorization documents which subdivide the contractual effort and responsibilities, within functional organizations?

253. Is each control account assigned to a single organizational element directly responsible for the work and identifiable to a single element of the CWBS?

254. Detailed schedules which support control account and work package start and completion dates/events?

255. Does the accounting system provide a basis for auditing records of direct costs chargeable to the contract?

256. Is the anticipated (firm and potential) business base Windows Defender Security Center projected in a rational, consistent manner?

257. Are current budgets resulting from changes to the authorized work and/or internal replanning, reconcilable to original budgets for specified reporting items?

2.10 Schedule Management Plan: Windows Defender Security Center

258. Is there an excessive and invalid use of task constraints and relationships of leads/lags?

259. Has the scope management document been updated and distributed to help prevent scope creep?

260. Are written status reports provided on a designated frequent basis?

261. Are risk triggers captured?

262. Is a process defined for baseline approval and control?

263. Does the ims include all contract and/or designated management control milestones?

264. Were Windows Defender Security Center project team members involved in the development of activity & task decomposition?

265. Was your organizations estimating methodology being used and followed?

266. Is there a formal process for updating the Windows Defender Security Center project baseline?

267. Are decisions captured in a decisions log?

268. Is the ims development and management

approach described?

269. Are meeting objectives identified for each meeting?

270. Does the Windows Defender Security Center project have a Statement of Work?

271. Are all payments made according to the contract(s)?

272. Does the time Windows Defender Security Center projection include an amount for contingencies (time reserves)?

273. Have all unresolved risks been documented?

274. Are Windows Defender Security Center project contact logs kept up to date?

275. Are staff skills known and available for each task?

276. Are risk oriented checklists used during risk identification?

2.11 Activity List: Windows Defender Security Center

277. Should you include sub-activities?

278. How do you determine the late start (LS) for each activity?

279. What is your organizations history in doing similar activities?

280. What is the total time required to complete the Windows Defender Security Center project if no delays occur?

281. For other activities, how much delay can be tolerated?

282. What is the probability the Windows Defender Security Center project can be completed in xx weeks?

283. How should ongoing costs be monitored to try to keep the Windows Defender Security Center project within budget?

284. What are you counting on?

285. What went well?

286. When will the work be performed?

287. Who will perform the work?

288. Are the required resources available or need to be acquired?

289. What went wrong?

290. How can the Windows Defender Security Center project be displayed graphically to better visualize the activities?

291. What did not go as well?

292. How will it be performed?

293. Can you determine the activity that must finish, before this activity can start?

294. Where will it be performed?

295. What is the LF and LS for each activity?

2.12 Activity Attributes: Windows Defender Security Center

296. What is missing?

297. What activity do you think you should spend the most time on?

298. Has management defined a definite timeframe for the turnaround or Windows Defender Security Center project window?

299. What is the general pattern here?

300. Resources to accomplish the work?

301. Would you consider either of corresponding activities an outlier?

302. Can you re-assign any activities to another resource to resolve an over-allocation?

303. Which method produces the more accurate cost assignment?

304. How else could the items be grouped?

305. Have constraints been applied to the start and finish milestones for the phases?

306. Are the required resources available?

307. Activity: what is In the Bag?

308. How difficult will it be to do specific activities on this Windows Defender Security Center project?

309. Is there a trend during the year?

310. Does your organization of the data change its meaning?

311. Time for overtime?

2.13 Milestone List: Windows Defender Security Center

312. Calculate how long can activity be delayed?

313. What are your competitors vulnerabilities?

314. Milestone pages should display the UserID of the person who added the milestone. Does a report or query exist that provides this audit information?

315. Timescales, deadlines and pressures?

316. Political effects?

317. Which path is the critical path?

318. Continuity, supply chain robustness?

319. How will the milestone be verified?

320. It is to be a narrative text providing the crucial aspects of your Windows Defender Security Center project proposal answering what, who, how, when and where?

321. Insurmountable weaknesses?

322. Environmental effects?

323. What background experience, skills, and strengths does the team bring to your organization?

324. How late can the activity start?

325. What date will the task finish?

326. Do you foresee any technical risks or developmental challenges?

327. Own known vulnerabilities?

328. Global influences?

329. Who will manage the Windows Defender Security Center project on a day-to-day basis?

2.14 Network Diagram: Windows Defender Security Center

330. Are you on time?

331. How difficult will it be to do specific activities on this Windows Defender Security Center project?

332. What job or jobs could run concurrently?

333. Will crashing x weeks return more in benefits than it costs?

334. What activity must be completed immediately before this activity can start?

335. What can be done concurrently?

336. What to do and When?

337. Why must you schedule milestones, such as reviews, throughout the Windows Defender Security Center project?

338. Are the gantt chart and/or network diagram updated periodically and used to assess the overall Windows Defender Security Center project timetable?

339. What activities must follow this activity?

340. What activities must occur simultaneously with this activity?

341. Which type of network diagram allows you to depict four types of dependencies?

342. Review the logical flow of the network diagram. Take a look at which activities you have first and then sequence the activities. Do they make sense?

343. How confident can you be in your milestone dates and the delivery date?

344. What is the lowest cost to complete this Windows Defender Security Center project in xx weeks?

345. What controls the start and finish of a job?

346. What are the tools?

347. What job or jobs precede it?

2.15 Activity Resource Requirements: Windows Defender Security Center

348. Are there unresolved issues that need to be addressed?

349. Is there anything planned that does not need to be here?

350. Why do you do that?

351. Which logical relationship does the PDM use most often?

352. Organizational Applicability?

353. Anything else?

354. Do you use tools like decomposition and rolling-wave planning to produce the activity list and other outputs?

355. What is the Work Plan Standard?

356. When does monitoring begin?

357. How many signatures do you require on a check and does this match what is in your policy and procedures?

358. What are constraints that you might find during the Human Resource Planning process?

359. How do you handle petty cash?

360. Other support in specific areas?

2.16 Resource Breakdown Structure: Windows Defender Security Center

361. What is the purpose of assigning and documenting responsibility?

362. Who needs what information?

363. Any changes from stakeholders?

364. What is the number one predictor of a groups productivity?

365. Why time management?

366. What are the requirements for resource data?

367. How can this help you with team building?

368. Which resource planning tool provides information on resource responsibility and accountability?

369. Who will use the system?

370. What is Windows Defender Security Center project communication management?

371. How difficult will it be to do specific activities on this Windows Defender Security Center project?

372. Who is allowed to perform which functions?

373. Goals for the Windows Defender Security Center project. What is each stakeholders desired outcome for the Windows Defender Security Center project?

374. What defines a successful Windows Defender Security Center project?

375. What is the difference between % Complete and % work?

376. Is predictive resource analysis being done?

377. Why is this important?

378. What is the primary purpose of the human resource plan?

2.17 Activity Duration Estimates: Windows Defender Security Center

379. Is corrective action taken to bring Windows Defender Security Center project performance into line with the Windows Defender Security Center project plan?

380. Which tips for taking the PMP exam do you think would be most helpful for you?

381. How could you define throughput and how would your organization benefit from maximizing it?

382. If you plan to take the PMP exam soon, what should you do to prepare?

383. Did anything besides luck make a difference between success and failure?

384. How can organizations use a weighted decision matrix to evaluate proposals as part of source selection?

385. How can software assist in Windows Defender Security Center project communications?

386. What are the ways to create and distribute Windows Defender Security Center project performance information?

387. How do theories relate to Windows Defender Security Center project management?

388. Are Windows Defender Security Center project costs tracked in the general ledger?

389. Which would be the NEXT thing for the Windows Defender Security Center project manager to do?

390. What functions does this software provide that cannot be done easily using other tools such as a spreadsheet or database?

391. What is earned value?

392. How does the job market and current state of the economy affect human resource management?

393. What are the three main outputs of quality control?

394. Are changes to the scope managed according to defined procedures?

395. Is action taken to increase the effectiveness and efficiency of Windows Defender Security Center projects?

396. What are key inputs and outputs of the software?

397. What distinguishes one organization from another in this area?

2.18 Duration Estimating Worksheet: Windows Defender Security Center

398. Small or large Windows Defender Security Center project?

399. Why estimate costs?

400. Done before proceeding with this activity or what can be done concurrently?

401. What info is needed?

402. What are the critical bottleneck activities?

403. Will the Windows Defender Security Center project collaborate with the local community and leverage resources?

404. When do the individual activities need to start and finish?

405. How can the Windows Defender Security Center project be displayed graphically to better visualize the activities?

406. When does your organization expect to be able to complete it?

407. What utility impacts are there?

408. When, then?

409. What is the total time required to complete the Windows Defender Security Center project if no delays occur?

410. What is your role?

411. Does the Windows Defender Security Center project provide innovative ways for stakeholders to overcome obstacles or deliver better outcomes?

412. Why estimate time and cost?

413. What work will be included in the Windows Defender Security Center project?

414. Do any colleagues have experience with your organization and/or RFPs?

2.19 Project Schedule: Windows Defender Security Center

415. How do you use schedules?

416. What is Windows Defender Security Center project management?

417. Did the Windows Defender Security Center project come in on schedule?

418. Meet requirements?

419. How can you fix it?

420. Is the structure for tracking the Windows Defender Security Center project schedule well defined and assigned to a specific individual?

421. How can slack be negative?

422. How do you manage Windows Defender Security Center project Risk?

423. What is the purpose of a Windows Defender Security Center project schedule?

424. Are quality inspections and review activities listed in the Windows Defender Security Center project schedule(s)?

425. What is risk?

426. Why is this particularly bad?

427. Change management required?

428. If there are any qualifying green components to this Windows Defender Security Center project, what portion of the total Windows Defender Security Center project cost is green?

429. What documents, if any, will the subcontractor provide (eg Windows Defender Security Center project schedule, quality plan etc)?

430. Is Windows Defender Security Center project work proceeding in accordance with the original Windows Defender Security Center project schedule?

431. Understand the constraints used in preparing the schedule. Are activities connected because logic dictates the order in which others occur?

432. How closely did the initial Windows Defender Security Center project Schedule compare with the actual schedule?

433. How much slack is available in the Windows Defender Security Center project?

2.20 Cost Management Plan: Windows Defender Security Center

434. What is Windows Defender Security Center project management?

435. Are the quality tools and methods identified in the Quality Plan appropriate to the Windows Defender Security Center project?

436. Time management – how will the schedule impact of changes be estimated and approved?

437. Quality assurance overheads?

438. Vac -variance at completion, how much over/under budget do you expect to be?

439. Have key stakeholders been identified?

440. Are non-critical path items updated and agreed upon with the teams?

441. Windows Defender Security Center project Objectives?

442. Have the key functions and capabilities been defined and assigned to each release or iteration?

443. Forecasts – how will the cost to complete the Windows Defender Security Center project be forecast?

444. Have external dependencies been captured in the schedule?

445. Is pert / critical path or equivalent methodology being used?

446. Are enough systems & user personnel assigned to the Windows Defender Security Center project?

447. Technical and functional?

448. Has Windows Defender Security Center project success criteria been defined?

449. Risk rating?

2.21 Activity Cost Estimates: Windows Defender Security Center

450. If you are asked to lower your estimate because the price is too high, what are your options?

451. What areas does the group agree are the biggest success on the Windows Defender Security Center project?

452. What were things that you need to improve?

453. Can you change your activities?

454. Based on your Windows Defender Security Center project communication management plan, what worked well?

455. How many activities should you have?

456. What is the estimators estimating history?

457. Estimated cost?

458. What is procurement?

459. Maintenance Reserve?

460. Can you delete activities or make them inactive?

461. Was the consultant knowledgeable about the program?

462. What is the Windows Defender Security Center projects sustainability strategy that will ensure Windows Defender Security Center project results will endure or be sustained?

463. Did the consultant work with local staff to develop local capacity?

464. What makes a good expected result statement?

465. What are you looking for?

466. What is the activity recast of the budget?

467. What is the activity inventory?

2.22 Cost Estimating Worksheet: Windows Defender Security Center

468. What costs are to be estimated?

469. Ask: are others positioned to know, are others credible, and will others cooperate?

470. Can a trend be established from historical performance data on the selected measure and are the criteria for using trend analysis or forecasting methods met?

471. What additional Windows Defender Security Center project(s) could be initiated as a result of this Windows Defender Security Center project?

472. What is the purpose of estimating?

473. Identify the timeframe necessary to monitor progress and collect data to determine how the selected measure has changed?

474. What can be included?

475. Is the Windows Defender Security Center project responsive to community need?

476. Is it feasible to establish a control group arrangement?

477. What will others want?

478. Who is best positioned to know and assist in identifying corresponding factors?

479. Will the Windows Defender Security Center project collaborate with the local community and leverage resources?

480. What is the estimated labor cost today based upon this information?

481. Does the Windows Defender Security Center project provide innovative ways for stakeholders to overcome obstacles or deliver better outcomes?

482. What happens to any remaining funds not used?

483. Value pocket identification & quantification what are value pockets?

484. How will the results be shared and to whom?

2.23 Cost Baseline: Windows Defender Security Center

485. What weaknesses do you have?

486. Why do you manage cost?

487. Are there contingencies or conditions related to the acceptance?

488. Does the suggested change request represent a desired enhancement to the products functionality?

489. Has the documentation relating to operation and maintenance of the product(s) or service(s) been delivered to, and accepted by, operations management?

490. How long are you willing to wait before you find out were late?

491. Definition of done can be traced back to the definitions of what are you providing to the customer in terms of deliverables?

492. Has operations management formally accepted responsibility for operating and maintaining the product(s) or service(s) delivered by the Windows Defender Security Center project?

493. What would the life cycle costs be?

494. Is there anything you need from upper

management in order to be successful?

495. What is the consequence?

496. Have all approved changes to the Windows Defender Security Center project requirement been identified and impact on the performance, cost, and schedule baselines documented?

497. On budget?

498. What strengths do you have?

499. Are you meeting with your team regularly?

500. Has the Windows Defender Security Center project (or Windows Defender Security Center project phase) been evaluated against each objective established in the product description and Integrated Windows Defender Security Center project Plan?

501. How difficult will it be to do specific tasks on the Windows Defender Security Center project?

502. How likely is it to go wrong?

503. If you sold 10x widgets on a day, what would the affect on profits be?

2.24 Quality Management Plan: Windows Defender Security Center

504. Who gets results of work?

505. What is the return on investment?

506. Have you eliminated all duplicative tasks or manual efforts, where appropriate?

507. Is the process working, and people are not executing in compliance of the process?

508. What are your results for key measures/indicators of accomplishment of organizational strategy?

509. Is a component/condition present?

510. What are your key performance measures/indicators for tracking progress relative to your action plans?

511. Do you periodically review your data quality system to see that it is up to date and appropriate?

512. Results Available?

513. Are there trends or hot spots?

514. Are there procedures in place to effectively manage interdependencies with other Windows Defender Security Center projects / systems?

515. Modifications to the requirements?

516. How do you measure?

517. How do you field-modify testing procedures?

518. What is quality and how will you ensure it?

519. What are the appropriate test methods to be used?

520. What would you gain if you spent time working to improve this process?

521. Who is responsible?

522. Meet how often?

523. Were the right locations/samples tested for the right parameters?

2.25 Quality Metrics: Windows Defender Security Center

524. What happens if you get an abnormal result?

525. The metrics–what is being considered?

526. Which report did you use to create the data you are submitting?

527. Is a risk containment plan in place?

528. Should a modifier be included?

529. Are there any open risk issues?

530. Subjective quality component: customer satisfaction, how do you measure it?

531. Has trace of defects been initiated?

532. Who notifies stakeholders of normal and abnormal results?

533. What are your organizations expectations for its quality Windows Defender Security Center project?

534. Does risk analysis documentation meet standards?

535. Where is quality now?

536. Where did complaints, returns and warranty

claims come from?

537. When will the Final Guidance will be issued?

538. What is the benchmark?

539. Do you know how much profit a 10% decrease in waste would generate?

540. What metrics are important and most beneficial to measure?

541. How do you communicate results and findings to upper management?

542. If the defect rate during testing is substantially higher than that of the previous release (or a similar product), then ask: Did you plan for and actually improve testing effectiveness?

543. What approved evidence based screening tools can be used?

2.26 Process Improvement Plan: Windows Defender Security Center

544. Have the frequency of collection and the points in the process where measurements will be made been determined?

545. If a process improvement framework is being used, which elements will help the problems and goals listed?

546. What lessons have you learned so far?

547. Does explicit definition of the measures exist?

548. Has the time line required to move measurement results from the points of collection to databases or users been established?

549. Where do you want to be?

550. Who should prepare the process improvement action plan?

551. Purpose of goal: the motive is determined by asking, why do you want to achieve this goal?

552. Have the supporting tools been developed or acquired?

553. To elicit goal statements, do you ask a question such as, What do you want to achieve?

554. Why do you want to achieve the goal?

555. The motive is determined by asking, Why do you want to achieve this goal?

556. Where are you now?

557. Are you meeting the quality standards?

558. Are you making progress on your improvement plan?

559. Are you making progress on the improvement framework?

560. What personnel are the coaches for your initiative?

561. What makes people good SPI coaches?

562. Does your process ensure quality?

2.27 Responsibility Assignment Matrix: Windows Defender Security Center

563. Availability – will the group or the person be available within the necessary time interval?

564. How many people do you need?

565. What will the work cost?

566. Are your organizations and items of cost assigned to each pool identified?

567. Do managers and team members provide helpful suggestions during review meetings?

568. Are the wbs and organizational levels for application of the Windows Defender Security Center projected overhead costs identified?

569. Are control accounts opened and closed based on the start and completion of work contained therein?

570. Is every signing-off responsibility and every communicating responsibility critically necessary?

571. Are there any drawbacks to using a responsibility assignment matrix?

572. The already stated responsible for overhead performance control of related costs?

573. Do you need to convince people that its well worth the time and effort?

574. Are work packages assigned to performing organizations?

575. Who is going to do that work?

576. All cwbs elements specified for external reporting?

577. Performance to date and material commitment?

578. Does the scheduling system identify in a timely manner the status of work?

579. Are the overhead pools formally and adequately identified?

580. Are estimates of costs at completion generated in a rational, consistent manner?

2.28 Roles and Responsibilities: Windows Defender Security Center

581. What expectations were NOT met?

582. What should you do now to prepare yourself for a promotion, increased responsibilities or a different job?

583. Who is involved?

584. Are governance roles and responsibilities documented?

585. What are your major roles and responsibilities in the area of performance measurement and assessment?

586. Implementation of actions: Who are the responsible units?

587. Was the expectation clearly communicated?

588. What is working well within your organizations performance management system?

589. What expectations were met?

590. Are Windows Defender Security Center project team roles and responsibilities identified and documented?

591. What should you do now to prepare for your

career 5+ years from now?

592. What should you do now to ensure that you are meeting all expectations of your current position?

593. Attainable / achievable: the goal is attainable; can you actually accomplish the goal?

594. What should you do now to ensure that you are exceeding expectations and excelling in your current position?

595. Who: who is involved?

596. Does your vision/mission support a culture of quality data?

597. Is there a training program in place for stakeholders covering expectations, roles and responsibilities and any addition knowledge others need to be good stakeholders?

598. To decide whether to use a quality measurement, ask how will you know when it is achieved?

599. Are your budgets supportive of a culture of quality data?

2.29 Human Resource Management Plan: Windows Defender Security Center

600. Are tasks tracked by hours?

601. Is there general agreement & acceptance of the current status and progress of the Windows Defender Security Center project?

602. Are the Windows Defender Security Center project team members located locally to the users/ stakeholders?

603. Where is your organization headed?

604. Does the schedule include Windows Defender Security Center project management time and change request analysis time?

605. Does all Windows Defender Security Center project documentation reside in a common repository for easy access?

606. Are quality inspections and review activities listed in the Windows Defender Security Center project schedule(s)?

607. Cost / benefit analysis?

608. Are milestone deliverables effectively tracked and compared to Windows Defender Security Center project plan?

609. Is current scope of the Windows Defender Security Center project substantially different than that originally defined?

610. Who needs training?

611. Is documentation created for communication with the suppliers and Vendors?

612. Are all key components of a Quality Assurance Plan present?

613. Are adequate resources provided for the quality assurance function?

614. What is this Windows Defender Security Center project aiming to achieve?

615. How does the proposed individual meet each requirement?

616. Does the Windows Defender Security Center project have a Statement of Work?

617. Has the Windows Defender Security Center project scope been baselined?

618. Personnel with expertise?

2.30 Communications Management Plan: Windows Defender Security Center

619. Who have you worked with in past, similar initiatives?

620. What is Windows Defender Security Center project communications management?

621. Do you ask; can you recommend others for you to talk with about this initiative?

622. Do you feel more overwhelmed by stakeholders?

623. Who to share with?

624. Which stakeholders can influence others?

625. How will the person responsible for executing the communication item be notified?

626. Conflict resolution -which method when?

627. What approaches do you use?

628. How were corresponding initiatives successful?

629. What help do you and your team need from the stakeholder?

630. What steps can you take for a positive relationship?

631. How did the term stakeholder originate?

632. Do you prepare stakeholder engagement plans?

633. Why is stakeholder engagement important?

634. What approaches to you feel are the best ones to use?

635. Who needs to know and how much?

636. Who are the members of the governing body?

637. What is the stakeholders level of authority?

2.31 Risk Management Plan: Windows Defender Security Center

638. Are the required plans included, such as nonstructural flood risk management plans?

639. How much risk protection can you afford?

640. Risk may be made during which step of risk management?

641. Is a software Windows Defender Security Center project management tool available?

642. Have you worked with the customer in the past?

643. What does a risk management program do?

644. Is the technology to be built new to your organization?

645. For software; does the software interface with new or unproven hardware or unproven vendor products?

646. Risk documentation: what reporting formats and processes will be used for risk management activities?

647. Are tool mentors available?

648. Are formal technical reviews part of this process?

649. Is Windows Defender Security Center project

scope stable?

650. Does the Windows Defender Security Center project have the authority and ability to avoid the risk?

651. Havent software Windows Defender Security Center projects been late before?

652. What would you do?

653. Have staff received necessary training?

654. Was an original risk assessment/risk management plan completed?

655. Are status updates being made on schedule and are the updates clearly described?

656. Can it be changed quickly?

2.32 Risk Register: Windows Defender Security Center

657. When is it going to be done?

658. Assume the risk event or situation happens, what would the impact be?

659. What is the probability and impact of the risk occurring?

660. Is further information required before making a decision?

661. What may happen or not go according to plan?

662. How are risks graded?

663. What action, if any, has been taken to respond to the risk?

664. What is a Community Risk Register?

665. How could corresponding Risk affect the Windows Defender Security Center project in terms of cost and schedule?

666. Having taken action, how did the responses effect change, and where is the Windows Defender Security Center project now?

667. Methodology: how will risk management be performed on this Windows Defender Security Center

project?

668. Schedule impact/severity estimated range (workdays) assume the event happens, what is the potential impact?

669. When would you develop a risk register?

670. Market risk -will the new service or product be useful to your organization or marketable to others?

671. What is a Risk?

672. What would the impact to the Windows Defender Security Center project objectives be should the risk arise?

673. Contingency actions - planned actions to reduce the immediate seriousness of the risk when it does occur. What should you do when?

674. Risk probability and impact: how will the probabilities and impacts of risk items be assessed?

675. User involvement: do you have the right users?

676. Are there other alternative controls that could be implemented?

2.33 Probability and Impact Assessment: Windows Defender Security Center

677. What is the likelihood?

678. What significant shift will occur in governmental policies, laws, and regulations pertaining to specific industries?

679. Do benefits and chances of success outweigh potential damage if success is not attained?

680. What are the likely future requirements?

681. What are your data sources?

682. What would be the effect of slippage?

683. Are the best people available?

684. Will new information become available during the Windows Defender Security Center project?

685. What is the likelihood of a breakthrough?

686. Which risks need to move on to Perform Quantitative Risk Analysis?

687. What should be the external organizations responsibility vis-à-vis total stake in the Windows Defender Security Center project?

688. How is the Windows Defender Security Center project going to be managed?

689. Which of your Windows Defender Security Center projects should be selected when compared with other Windows Defender Security Center projects?

690. Do you train all developers in the process?

691. Monitoring of the overall Windows Defender Security Center project status – are there any changes in the Windows Defender Security Center project that can effect and cause new possible risks?

692. How do you define a risk?

693. Are there alternative opinions/solutions/processes you should explore?

694. Risk data quality assessment - what is the quality of the data used to determine or assess the risk?

695. Assumptions analysis -what assumptions have you made or been given about your Windows Defender Security Center project?

2.34 Probability and Impact Matrix: Windows Defender Security Center

696. Do the people have the right combinations of skills?

697. How realistic is the timing of introduction?

698. Risk categorization -which of your categories has more risk than others?

699. What should be done with risks on the watch list?

700. Have top software and customer managers formally committed to support the Windows Defender Security Center project?

701. My Windows Defender Security Center project leader has suddenly left your organization, what do you do?

702. Can you handle the investment risk?

703. Are enough people available?

704. During Windows Defender Security Center project executing, a major problem occurs that was not included in the risk register. What should you do FIRST?

705. Can it be enlarged by drawing people from other areas of your organization?

706. Who has experience with this?

707. What will be the environmental impact of the Windows Defender Security Center project?

708. What is the probability of the risk occurring?

709. Is the customer willing to participate in reviews?

710. What can possibly go wrong?

711. Brain storm – mind maps, what if?

712. How solid is the Windows Defender Security Center projection of competitive reaction?

713. Does the Windows Defender Security Center project team have experience with the technology to be implemented?

714. Are the risk data complete?

715. Is the customer technically sophisticated in the product area?

2.35 Risk Data Sheet: Windows Defender Security Center

716. Risk of what?

717. Is the data sufficiently specified in terms of the type of failure being analyzed, and its frequency or probability?

718. How reliable is the data source?

719. What do you know?

720. What are you here for (Mission)?

721. What will be the consequences if it happens?

722. What is the chance that it will happen?

723. Has the most cost-effective solution been chosen?

724. What do people affected think about the need for, and practicality of preventive measures?

725. What is the environment within which you operate (social trends, economic, community values, broad based participation, national directions etc.)?

726. How can it happen?

727. What actions can be taken to eliminate or remove risk?

728. What if client refuses?

729. What can happen?

730. How do you handle product safely?

731. What was measured?

732. What will be the consequences if the risk happens?

733. What are you weak at and therefore need to do better?

734. Has a sensitivity analysis been carried out?

735. What is the likelihood of it happening?

2.36 Procurement Management Plan: Windows Defender Security Center

736. Are Windows Defender Security Center project team members involved in detailed estimating and scheduling?

737. Is the Windows Defender Security Center project sponsor clearly communicating the business case or rationale for why this Windows Defender Security Center project is needed?

738. Are updated Windows Defender Security Center project time & resource estimates reasonable based on the current Windows Defender Security Center project stage?

739. In which phase of the Acquisition Process Cycle does source qualifications reside?

740. Does all Windows Defender Security Center project documentation reside in a common repository for easy access?

741. What are you trying to accomplish?

742. Does the schedule include Windows Defender Security Center project management time and change request analysis time?

743. Were sponsors and decision makers available when needed outside regularly scheduled meetings?

744. What is the last item a Windows Defender Security Center project manager must do to finalize Windows Defender Security Center project close-out?

745. Is the schedule updated on a periodic basis?

746. Is there a requirements change management processes in place?

747. How will the duration of the Windows Defender Security Center project influence your decisions?

748. Are quality metrics defined?

749. Why do you do it?

750. Has a structured approach been used to break work effort into manageable components (WBS)?

751. Is there an issues management plan in place?

752. Are mitigation strategies identified?

753. Are stakeholders aware and supportive of the principles and practices of modern software estimation?

2.37 Source Selection Criteria: Windows Defender Security Center

754. Are types/quantities of material, facilities appropriate?

755. How should oral presentations be prepared for?

756. What should clarifications include?

757. What management structure does your organization consider as optimal for performing the contract?

758. Which contract type places the most risk on the seller?

759. What are the guidelines regarding award without considerations?

760. How long will it take for the purchase cost to be the same as the lease cost?

761. Is the contracting office likely to receive more purchase requests for this item or service during the coming year?

762. Are there any common areas of weaknesses or deficiencies in the proposals in the competitive range?

763. How should the preproposal conference be conducted?

764. Are responses to considerations adequate?

765. Is there collaboration among your evaluators?

766. Do you want to have them collaborate at subfactor level?

767. Have team members been adequately trained?

768. If the costs are normalized, please account for how the normalization is conducted. Is a cost realism analysis used?

769. What source selection software is your team using?

770. Have all evaluators been trained?

771. What instructions should be provided regarding oral presentations?

772. What should be considered when developing evaluation standards?

773. Do you ensure you evaluate what you asked for, not what you want to see or expect to see?

2.38 Stakeholder Management Plan: Windows Defender Security Center

774. Is a payment system in place with proper reviews and approvals?

775. What training requirements are there based upon the required skills and resources?

776. Was trending evident between audits?

777. Does the system design reflect the requirements?

778. Are Windows Defender Security Center project contact logs kept up to date?

779. Who will be collecting information?

780. Are the schedule estimates reasonable given the Windows Defender Security Center project?

781. Will all relevant stakeholders be included within the review process?

782. Pareto diagrams, statistical sampling, flow charting or trend analysis used quality monitoring?

783. Have process improvement efforts been completed before requirements efforts begin?

784. Who is responsible for the post implementation review process?

785. Is there a Steering Committee in place?

786. Are there unnecessary steps that are creating bottlenecks and/or causing people to wait?

787. Is a pmo (Windows Defender Security Center project management office) in place and does it provide oversight to the Windows Defender Security Center project?

788. What is meant by managing the triple constraint?

789. Is the current scope of the Windows Defender Security Center project substantially different than that originally defined?

2.39 Change Management Plan: Windows Defender Security Center

790. Will you need new processes?

791. What are the dependencies?

792. Why is it important?

793. What are the training strategies?

794. What work practices will be affected?

795. What are the major changes to processes?

796. What goal(s) do you hope to accomplish?

797. Do you need new systems?

798. What did the people around you say about it?

799. What will be the preferred method of delivery?

800. Where will the funds come from?

801. What risks may occur upfront, during implementation and after implementation?

802. When should a given message be communicated?

803. What policies and procedures need to be changed?

804. Who should be involved in developing a change management strategy?

805. What provokes organizational change?

806. Is there a need for new relationships to be built?

807. What is the worst thing that can happen if you communicate information?

3.0 Executing Process Group: Windows Defender Security Center

808. How many different communication channels does the Windows Defender Security Center project team have?

809. Does the case present a realistic scenario?

810. What does it mean to take a systems view of a Windows Defender Security Center project?

811. How will you avoid scope creep?

812. What is the difference between conceptual, application, and evaluative questions?

813. In what way has the program come up with innovative measures for problem-solving?

814. What are the challenges Windows Defender Security Center project teams face?

815. If a risk event occurs, what will you do?

816. Who will be the main sponsor?

817. Just how important is your work to the overall success of the Windows Defender Security Center project?

818. How do you measure difficulty?

819. Are escalated issues resolved promptly?

820. What areas were overlooked on this Windows Defender Security Center project?

821. What are the typical Windows Defender Security Center project management skills?

822. Will additional funds be needed for hardware or software?

823. Is the Windows Defender Security Center project performing better or worse than planned?

824. Is the schedule for the set products being met?

825. Are decisions made in a timely manner?

3.1 Team Member Status Report: Windows Defender Security Center

826. Does your organization have the means (staff, money, contract, etc.) to produce or to acquire the product, good, or service?

827. What is to be done?

828. What specific interest groups do you have in place?

829. How can you make it practical?

830. How does this product, good, or service meet the needs of the Windows Defender Security Center project and your organization as a whole?

831. The problem with Reward & Recognition Programs is that the truly deserving people all too often get left out. How can you make it practical?

832. How it is to be done?

833. Does the product, good, or service already exist within your organization?

834. Are your organizations Windows Defender Security Center projects more successful over time?

835. How will resource planning be done?

836. When a teams productivity and success depend

on collaboration and the efficient flow of information, what generally fails them?

837. Will the staff do training or is that done by a third party?

838. How much risk is involved?

839. Does every department have to have a Windows Defender Security Center project Manager on staff?

840. Are the attitudes of staff regarding Windows Defender Security Center project work improving?

841. Do you have an Enterprise Windows Defender Security Center project Management Office (EPMO)?

842. Is there evidence that staff is taking a more professional approach toward management of your organizations Windows Defender Security Center projects?

843. Why is it to be done?

844. Are the products of your organizations Windows Defender Security Center projects meeting customers objectives?

3.2 Change Request: Windows Defender Security Center

845. How fast will change requests be approved?

846. How many times must the change be modified or presented to the change control board before it is approved?

847. Who is responsible to authorize changes?

848. Have all related configuration items been properly updated?

849. Why were your requested changes rejected or not made?

850. Can static requirements change attributes like the size of the change be used to predict reliability in execution?

851. What kind of information about the change request needs to be captured?

852. Screen shots or attachments included in a Change Request?

853. Who is included in the change control team?

854. What has an inspector to inspect and to check?

855. Have scm procedures for noting the change, recording it, and reporting it been followed?

856. When do you create a change request?

857. What should be regulated in a change control operating instruction?

858. Can you answer what happened, who did it, when did it happen, and what else will be affected?

859. What is the relationship between requirements attributes and reliability?

860. What is the purpose of change control?

861. Change request coordination ?

862. How does your organization control changes before and after software is released to a customer?

863. Are there requirements attributes that are strongly related to the complexity and size?

864. Will all change requests and current status be logged?

3.3 Change Log: Windows Defender Security Center

865. How does this change affect the timeline of the schedule?

866. When was the request approved?

867. Is the change backward compatible without limitations?

868. Is the change request open, closed or pending?

869. Do the described changes impact on the integrity or security of the system?

870. How does this relate to the standards developed for specific business processes?

871. How does this change affect scope?

872. Is the submitted change a new change or a modification of a previously approved change?

873. Is this a mandatory replacement?

874. Does the suggested change request seem to represent a necessary enhancement to the product?

875. Where do changes come from?

876. Is the change request within Windows Defender Security Center project scope?

877. Who initiated the change request?

878. Should a more thorough impact analysis be conducted?

879. Is the requested change request a result of changes in other Windows Defender Security Center project(s)?

880. Will the Windows Defender Security Center project fail if the change request is not executed?

881. When was the request submitted?

3.4 Decision Log: Windows Defender Security Center

882. Do strategies and tactics aimed at less than full control reduce the costs of management or simply shift the cost burden?

883. Meeting purpose; why does this team meet?

884. How does provision of information, both in terms of content and presentation, influence acceptance of alternative strategies?

885. How do you know when you are achieving it?

886. Behaviors; what are guidelines that the team has identified that will assist them with getting the most out of team meetings?

887. Linked to original objective?

888. At what point in time does loss become unacceptable?

889. Decision-making process; how will the team make decisions?

890. With whom was the decision shared or considered?

891. Which variables make a critical difference?

892. Who will be given a copy of this document and

where will it be kept?

893. Is everything working as expected?

894. What was the rationale for the decision?

895. How does an increasing emphasis on cost containment influence the strategies and tactics used?

896. What eDiscovery problem or issue did your organization set out to fix or make better?

897. Is your opponent open to a non-traditional workflow, or will it likely challenge anything you do?

898. What is your overall strategy for quality control / quality assurance procedures?

899. Who is the decisionmaker?

900. Does anything need to be adjusted?

901. How effective is maintaining the log at facilitating organizational learning?

3.5 Quality Audit: Windows Defender Security Center

902. What happens if your organization fails its Quality Audit?

903. How does your organization know that its system for attending to the health and wellbeing of its staff is appropriately effective and constructive?

904. Are multiple statements on the same issue consistent with each other?

905. Do prior clients have a positive opinion of your organization?

906. Have personnel cleanliness and health requirements been established?

907. How does your organization know that its relationships with other relevant organizations are appropriately effective and constructive?

908. How does your organization know that its staff placements are appropriately effective and constructive in relation to program-related learning outcomes?

909. Is refuse and garbage adequately stored and disposed of with sufficient frequency to prevent contamination?

910. How does your organization know that its

system for staff performance planning and review is appropriately effective and constructive?

911. Is your organizational structure established and each positions responsibility defined?

912. Will the evidence likely be sufficient and appropriate?

913. How does your organization know that it is effectively and constructively guiding staff through to timely completion of tasks?

914. Is quality audit a prerequisite for program accreditation or program recognition?

915. Are adequate and conveniently located toilet facilities available for use by the employees?

916. Does the report read coherently?

917. Are all areas associated with the storage and reconditioning of devices clean, free of rubbish, adequately ventilated and in good repair?

918. Has a written procedure been established to identify devices during all stages of receipt, reconditioning, distribution and installation so that mix-ups are prevented?

919. How does your organization know that its systems for communicating with and among staff are appropriately effective and constructive?

920. How does your organization know that its system for recruiting the best staff possible are appropriately

effective and constructive?

921. How does your organization know that its quality of teaching is appropriately effective and constructive?

3.6 Team Directory: Windows Defender Security Center

922. Process decisions: are there any statutory or regulatory issues relevant to the timely execution of work?

923. Why is the work necessary?

924. Process decisions: which organizational elements and which individuals will be assigned management functions?

925. Decisions: what could be done better to improve the quality of the constructed product?

926. Process decisions: do invoice amounts match accepted work in place?

927. Days from the time the issue is identified?

928. How do unidentified risks impact the outcome of the Windows Defender Security Center project?

929. How will the team handle changes?

930. Process decisions: is work progressing on schedule and per contract requirements?

931. Who will write the meeting minutes and distribute?

932. How and in what format should information be

presented?

933. Who will talk to the customer?

934. How will you accomplish and manage the objectives?

935. Contract requirements complied with?

936. What are you going to deliver or accomplish?

937. Process decisions: are all start-up, turn over and close out requirements of the contract satisfied?

938. Process decisions: are contractors adequately prosecuting the work?

939. Process decisions: do job conditions warrant additional actions to collect job information and document on-site activity?

940. Who are your stakeholders (customers, sponsors, end users, team members)?

3.7 Team Operating Agreement: Windows Defender Security Center

941. What are some potential sources of conflict among team members?

942. Are there the right people on your team?

943. Do you post any action items, due dates, and responsibilities on the team website?

944. Are leadership responsibilities shared among team members (versus a single leader)?

945. Do you record meetings for the already stated unable to attend?

946. What are the boundaries (organizational or geographic) within which you operate?

947. Do you brief absent members after they view meeting notes or listen to a recording?

948. How do you want to be thought of and known within your organization?

949. Did you determine the technology methods that best match the messages to be communicated?

950. To whom do you deliver your services?

951. Must your team members rely on the expertise of other members to complete tasks?

952. Confidentiality: how will confidential information be handled?

953. What individual strengths does each team member bring to the group?

954. Are there more than two functional areas represented by your team?

955. Does your team need access to all documents and information at all times?

956. Have you established procedures that team members can follow to work effectively together, such as a team operating agreement?

957. Reimbursements: how will the team members be reimbursed for expenses and time commitments?

958. Do you solicit member feedback about meetings and what would make them better?

959. How will you divide work equitably?

960. What is your unique contribution to your organization?

3.8 Team Performance Assessment: Windows Defender Security Center

961. To what degree are the goals ambitious?

962. To what degree do team members frequently explore the teams purpose and its implications?

963. Does more radicalness mean more perceived benefits?

964. To what degree are staff involved as partners in the improvement process?

965. To what degree are fresh input and perspectives systematically caught and added (for example, through information and analysis, new members, and senior sponsors)?

966. To what degree do team members agree with the goals, relative importance, and the ways in which achievement will be measured?

967. To what degree are the members clear on what they are individually responsible for and what they are jointly responsible for?

968. To what degree does the teams approach to its work allow for modification and improvement over time?

969. What makes opportunities more or less obvious?

970. How do you encourage members to learn from each other?

971. To what degree can all members engage in open and interactive considerations?

972. When does the medium matter?

973. Can team performance be reliably measured in simulator and live exercises using the same assessment tool?

974. To what degree can the team measure progress against specific goals?

975. How does Windows Defender Security Center project termination impact Windows Defender Security Center project team members?

976. Social categorization and intergroup behaviour: Does minimal intergroup discrimination make social identity more positive?

977. To what degree can team members vigorously define the teams purpose in considerations with others who are not part of the functioning team?

978. To what degree is there a sense that only the team can succeed?

979. If you have received criticism from reviewers that your work suffered from method variance, what was the circumstance?

980. To what degree will team members, individually and collectively, commit time to help themselves and

others learn and develop skills?

3.9 Team Member Performance Assessment: Windows Defender Security Center

981. How is performance assessment used in making future award decisions including options and extend/compete decisions?

982. What are the basic principles and objectives of performance measurement and assessment?

983. To what degree are the goals realistic?

984. What instructional strategies were developed/incorporated (e.g., direct instruction, indirect instruction, experiential learning, independent study, interactive instruction)?

985. What qualities does a successful Team leader possess?

986. How does your team work together?

987. What are the staffs preferences for training on technology-based platforms?

988. Has the appropriate access to relevant data and analysis capability been granted?

989. What types of learning are targeted (e.g., cognitive, affective, psychomotor, procedural)?

990. Why do performance reviews?

991. How will they be formed?

992. Is it clear how goals will be accomplished?

993. Is it critical or vital to the job?

994. What are acceptable governance changes?

995. How do you start collaborating?

996. What kinds of performance factors / elements do you use?

997. How do you create a self-sustaining capacity for a collaborative culture?

998. How accurately is your plan implemented?

999. To what degree is the team cognizant of small wins to be celebrated along the way?

1000. Should a ratee get a copy of all the raters documents about the employees performance?

3.10 Issue Log: Windows Defender Security Center

1001. Who is the stakeholder?

1002. Where do team members get information?

1003. How much time does it take to do it?

1004. Who is the issue assigned to?

1005. What is the status of the issue?

1006. Are the Windows Defender Security Center project issues uniquely identified, including to which product they refer?

1007. How is this initiative related to other portfolios, programs, or Windows Defender Security Center projects?

1008. Why do you manage communications?

1009. What help do you and your team need from the stakeholders?

1010. Who reported the issue?

1011. How do you manage human resources?

1012. Are stakeholder roles recognized by your organization?

1013. Are there common objectives between the team and the stakeholder?

1014. Are there potential barriers between the team and the stakeholder?

1015. What effort will a change need?

1016. What is a change?

1017. Is the issue log kept in a safe place?

4.0 Monitoring and Controlling Process Group: Windows Defender Security Center

1018. Mitigate. what will you do to minimize the impact should a risk event occur?

1019. Who needs to be involved in the planning?

1020. Change, where should you look for problems?

1021. How many potential communications channels exist on the Windows Defender Security Center project?

1022. What is the expected monetary value of the Windows Defender Security Center project?

1023. What factors are contributing to progress or delay in the achievement of products and results?

1024. What input will you be required to provide the Windows Defender Security Center project team?

1025. Is there undesirable impact on staff or resources?

1026. How is agile portfolio management done?

1027. Propriety: who needs to be involved in the evaluation to be ethical?

1028. How can you make your needs known?

1029. Did the Windows Defender Security Center project team have the right skills?

1030. How to ensure validity, quality and consistency?

1031. Did it work?

1032. What is the timeline?

1033. How can you monitor progress?

1034. Do the products created live up to the necessary quality?

1035. What communication items need improvement?

1036. Overall, how does the program function to serve the clients?

4.1 Project Performance Report: Windows Defender Security Center

1037. To what degree do the relationships of the informal organization motivate taskrelevant behavior and facilitate task completion?

1038. To what degree can the cognitive capacity of individuals accommodate the flow of information?

1039. How can Windows Defender Security Center project sustainability be maintained?

1040. To what degree does the teams purpose contain themes that are particularly meaningful and memorable?

1041. To what degree will new and supplemental skills be introduced as the need is recognized?

1042. To what degree do team members articulate the teams work approach?

1043. To what degree will the approach capitalize on and enhance the skills of all team members in a manner that takes into consideration other demands on members of the team?

1044. To what degree are the demands of the task compatible with and converge with the mission and functions of the formal organization?

1045. To what degree are the demands of the task

compatible with and converge with the relationships of the informal organization?

1046. What is in it for you?

1047. To what degree do members articulate the goals beyond the team membership?

1048. To what degree does the information network communicate information relevant to the task?

1049. To what degree do team members understand one anothers roles and skills?

1050. To what degree does the informal organization make use of individual resources and meet individual needs?

1051. To what degree do the goals specify concrete team work products?

1052. To what degree does the teams work approach provide opportunity for members to engage in results-based evaluation?

4.2 Variance Analysis: Windows Defender Security Center

1053. What is the expected future profitability of each customer?

1054. Did a new competitor enter the market?

1055. What should management do?

1056. Are overhead cost budgets established for each department which has authority to incur overhead costs?

1057. Are indirect costs accumulated for comparison with the corresponding budgets?

1058. Does the contractors system include procedures for measuring the performance of critical subcontractors?

1059. Are the wbs and organizational levels for application of the Windows Defender Security Center projected overhead costs identified?

1060. What does an unfavorable overhead volume variance mean?

1061. Why do variances exist?

1062. Can the contractor substantiate work package and planning package budgets?

1063. Is there a logical explanation for any variance?

1064. Is cost and schedule performance measurement done in a consistent, systematic manner?

1065. What was the cause of the increase in costs?

1066. Can process improvements lead to unfavorable variances?

1067. Contemplated overhead expenditure for each period based on the best information currently is available?

1068. Is the entire contract planned in time-phased control accounts to the extent practicable?

1069. What is the actual cost of work performed?

1070. Does the contractor use objective results, design reviews and tests to trace schedule performance?

4.3 Earned Value Status: Windows Defender Security Center

1071. What is the unit of forecast value?

1072. Earned value can be used in almost any Windows Defender Security Center project situation and in almost any Windows Defender Security Center project environment. it may be used on large Windows Defender Security Center projects, medium sized Windows Defender Security Center projects, tiny Windows Defender Security Center projects (in cut-down form), complex and simple Windows Defender Security Center projects and in any market sector. some people, of course, know all about earned value, they have used it for years - but perhaps not as effectively as they could have?

1073. Verification is a process of ensuring that the developed system satisfies the stakeholders agreements and specifications; Are you building the product right? What do you verify?

1074. Are you hitting your Windows Defender Security Center projects targets?

1075. Where is evidence-based earned value in your organization reported?

1076. Where are your problem areas?

1077. Validation is a process of ensuring that the developed system will actually achieve the stakeholders desired outcomes; Are you building the right product? What do you validate?

1078. How does this compare with other Windows Defender Security Center projects?

1079. How much is it going to cost by the finish?

1080. When is it going to finish?

1081. If earned value management (EVM) is so good in determining the true status of a Windows Defender Security Center project and Windows Defender Security Center project its completion, why is it that hardly any one uses it in information systems related Windows Defender Security Center projects?

4.4 Risk Audit: Windows Defender Security Center

1082. Will an appropriate standard of care be applied to all involved?

1083. Does the implementation method matter?

1084. Is your organization able to present documentary evidence in support of compliance?

1085. Are all managers or operators of the facility or equipment competent or qualified?

1086. What are the strategic implications with clients when auditors focus audit resources based on business-level risks?

1087. What is the anticipated volatility of the requirements?

1088. Are some people working on multiple Windows Defender Security Center projects?

1089. Do you have proper induction processes for all new paid staff and volunteers who have a specific role and responsibility?

1090. Have top software and customer managers formally committed to support the Windows Defender Security Center project?

1091. Number of users of the product?

1092. Are policies communicated to all affected?

1093. Is there a screening process that will ensure all participants have the fitness and skills required to safely participate?

1094. Does the customer understand the process?

1095. Are the software tools integrated with each other?

1096. Do you have a mechanism for managing change?

1097. Are you willing to seek legal advice when required?

1098. Is a software Windows Defender Security Center project management tool available?

1099. What are the risks that could stop you from achieving your KPIs?

1100. Do industry specialists and business risk auditors enhance audit reporting accuracy?

4.5 Contractor Status Report: Windows Defender Security Center

1101. What was the budget or estimated cost for your organizations services?

1102. What was the final actual cost?

1103. How long have you been using the services?

1104. Describe how often regular updates are made to the proposed solution. Are corresponding regular updates included in the standard maintenance plan?

1105. What process manages the contracts?

1106. Are there contractual transfer concerns?

1107. What is the average response time for answering a support call?

1108. What was the overall budget or estimated cost?

1109. Who can list a Windows Defender Security Center project as organization experience, your organization or a previous employee of your organization?

1110. What are the minimum and optimal bandwidth requirements for the proposed solution?

1111. How is risk transferred?

1112. What was the actual budget or estimated cost for your organizations services?

1113. If applicable; describe your standard schedule for new software version releases. Are new software version releases included in the standard maintenance plan?

4.6 Formal Acceptance: Windows Defender Security Center

1114. Who would use it?

1115. Do you buy-in installation services?

1116. Does it do what Windows Defender Security Center project team said it would?

1117. Did the Windows Defender Security Center project manager and team act in a professional and ethical manner?

1118. Do you perform formal acceptance or burn-in tests?

1119. What is the Acceptance Management Process?

1120. Does it do what client said it would?

1121. What can you do better next time?

1122. What lessons were learned about your Windows Defender Security Center project management methodology?

1123. What features, practices, and processes proved to be strengths or weaknesses?

1124. What function(s) does it fill or meet?

1125. Was the client satisfied with the Windows

Defender Security Center project results?

1126. Is formal acceptance of the Windows Defender Security Center project product documented and distributed?

1127. What are the requirements against which to test, Who will execute?

1128. General estimate of the costs and times to complete the Windows Defender Security Center project?

1129. Do you buy pre-configured systems or build your own configuration?

1130. Who supplies data?

1131. Was the sponsor/customer satisfied?

1132. Was business value realized?

1133. Was the Windows Defender Security Center project work done on time, within budget, and according to specification?

5.0 Closing Process Group: Windows Defender Security Center

1134. What business situation is being addressed?

1135. What were things that you did well, and could improve, and how?

1136. What areas were overlooked on this Windows Defender Security Center project?

1137. Is the Windows Defender Security Center project funded?

1138. Is there a clear cause and effect between the activity and the lesson learned?

1139. How well did the chosen processes fit the needs of the Windows Defender Security Center project?

1140. Can the lesson learned be replicated?

1141. Were risks identified and mitigated?

1142. What can you do better next time, and what specific actions can you take to improve?

1143. Does the close educate others to improve performance?

1144. Were escalated issues resolved promptly?

1145. Did the delivered product meet the specified

requirements and goals of the Windows Defender Security Center project?

1146. What were things that you did very well and want to do the same again on the next Windows Defender Security Center project?

1147. Were cost budgets met?

1148. How dependent is the Windows Defender Security Center project on other Windows Defender Security Center projects or work efforts?

1149. What is the risk of failure to your organization?

5.1 Procurement Audit: Windows Defender Security Center

1150. Who had not previously applied to participate?

1151. How do you monitor behaviour of procurement staff?

1152. Are travel expenditures monitored to determine that they are in line with other employees and reasonable for the area of travel?

1153. Are transportation charges verified?

1154. Are copies of policies made available to staff members involved in budget preparation and administration?

1155. Is it calculated whether aggregated procurement can be more cost-efficient?

1156. Does the procurement function/unit have the ability to negotiate with customers and suppliers?

1157. Is there a policy covering the relationship of other departments with vendors?

1158. Does procurement staff have recognized professional procurement qualifications or sufficient training?

1159. Is your organization transparent about winning bids and prices?

1160. Must the receipt of goods be approved prior to payment?

1161. Were additional works strictly necessary for the completion of performance under the contract?

1162. Was the pre-qualification screening for issue of tender documents done properly and in a fair manner?

1163. Where an electronic auction was used to bid, were all required specifications given equally to tenderers?

1164. Do the internal control systems function appropriate?

1165. Is there management monitoring of transactions and balances?

1166. Were additional works charged at the unit prices agreed in the initial contract?

1167. Are all purchase orders reviewed by someone other than the individual preparing the purchase order (reasonableness of order and vendor selection)?

1168. Is sufficient evidence required for all disbursements (except nominal amounts)?

1169. Are there any complaints of the suppliers and/or end-users?

5.2 Contract Close-Out: Windows Defender Security Center

1170. What is capture management?

1171. Have all contract records been included in the Windows Defender Security Center project archives?

1172. Has each contract been audited to verify acceptance and delivery?

1173. Was the contract type appropriate?

1174. Change in knowledge?

1175. Have all contracts been completed?

1176. Change in circumstances?

1177. Change in attitude or behavior?

1178. Have all contracts been closed?

1179. Have all acceptance criteria been met prior to final payment to contractors?

1180. How does it work?

1181. Parties: who is involved?

1182. How/when used ?

1183. How is the contracting office notified of the

automatic contract close-out?

1184. Are the signers the authorized officials?

1185. Was the contract complete without requiring numerous changes and revisions?

1186. Parties: Authorized?

1187. What happens to the recipient of services?

1188. Was the contract sufficiently clear so as not to result in numerous disputes and misunderstandings?

5.3 Project or Phase Close-Out: Windows Defender Security Center

1189. Did the Windows Defender Security Center project management methodology work?

1190. What were the goals and objectives of the communications strategy for the Windows Defender Security Center project?

1191. What are they?

1192. What are the mandatory communication needs for each stakeholder?

1193. What was expected from each stakeholder?

1194. Is the lesson significant, valid, and applicable?

1195. What could have been improved?

1196. What were the desired outcomes?

1197. Planned completion date?

1198. Did the delivered product meet the specified requirements and goals of the Windows Defender Security Center project?

1199. Who exerted influence that has positively affected or negatively impacted the Windows Defender Security Center project?

1200. What was learned?

1201. What hierarchical authority does the stakeholder have in your organization?

1202. What is the information level of detail required for each stakeholder?

1203. What benefits or impacts does the stakeholder group expect to obtain as a result of the Windows Defender Security Center project?

1204. Have business partners been involved extensively, and what data was required for them?

1205. Who are the Windows Defender Security Center project stakeholders and what are roles and involvement?

1206. What are the informational communication needs for each stakeholder?

5.4 Lessons Learned: Windows Defender Security Center

1207. Was there a Windows Defender Security Center project Definition document. Was there a Windows Defender Security Center project Plan. Were they used during the Windows Defender Security Center project?

1208. If you had to do this Windows Defender Security Center project again, what is the one thing that you would change (related to process, not to technical solutions)?

1209. Did the delivered product meet the specified requirements and goals of the Windows Defender Security Center project?

1210. How many government and contractor personnel are authorized for the Windows Defender Security Center project?

1211. Does the lesson describe a function that would be done differently the next time?

1212. How effective was the acceptance management process?

1213. How effectively and consistently was sponsorship for the Windows Defender Security Center project conveyed?

1214. What would you like to see better documented

about how to use existing processes on this type of Windows Defender Security Center project?

1215. What skills did you need that were missing on this Windows Defender Security Center project?

1216. What worked well?

1217. Was the control overhead justified?

1218. How efficient and effective were Windows Defender Security Center project team meetings?

1219. What was the geopolitical history during the origin of your organization and at the time of task input?

1220. What things mattered the most on this Windows Defender Security Center project?

1221. How effective was the documentation that you received with the Windows Defender Security Center project product/service?

1222. Were any strategies or activities unsuccessful?

1223. What skills are required for the task?

1224. What is your strategy for data collection?

1225. What were the main bottlenecks on the process?

1226. What is your organizations performance history?

Index

ability 40, 83, 202, 259
abnormal   189
absent 234
acceptable   52, 89, 100, 240
acceptance 7, 122, 185, 197, 227, 255-256, 261, 265
accepted   128, 140, 185, 232
access 2, 8-10, 26, 72, 136, 145, 197, 211, 235, 239
accomplish   8, 87, 110, 126, 163, 196, 211, 217, 233
accordance   178
according   42, 150, 160, 174, 203, 256
account   35, 55, 157, 214
accounting   157
accounts   156, 193, 248
accrue 141
accuracy   252
accurate   10, 117, 163
accurately   240
achievable   115, 196
achieve   8, 65, 81, 118, 191-192, 198, 249
achieved   22, 77, 114, 196
achieving   227, 252
acquire   221
acquired   162, 191
across 46
action 44, 46, 94, 96, 98, 101, 138, 150, 153, 157, 173-174, 187, 191, 203, 234
actionable   55, 113
actions 18, 101, 151, 195, 204, 209, 233, 257
active 152
activities   18, 25, 38, 85, 91, 102, 111, 144, 161-164, 167-168, 171, 175, 177-178, 181, 197, 201, 266
activity 3-4, 34, 41, 138, 143, 152, 157, 159, 161-163, 165-167, 169, 173, 175, 181-182, 233, 257
actual 34, 57, 178, 248, 253-254
actually   38, 61, 82, 97, 190, 196, 249
adapted   138
addition   107, 196
additional   30-31, 61, 70, 72-73, 183, 220, 233, 260
additions   99
address   17, 76, 139

268

addressed		169, 257
addressing		40, 109
adequate		30, 198, 214, 230
adequately		30, 139, 194, 214, 229-230, 233
adjust 92
adjusted		102, 228
advantage		65, 106
advantages		105
advice 252
affect 63, 66-67, 108, 136, 143, 148, 151, 174, 186, 203, 225
affected		142, 209, 217, 224, 252, 263
affecting		12, 20, 62
affective		239
afford 201
against 39, 95, 102, 186, 237, 256
agenda		139
agendas		116
aggregate		46
aggregated		259
agreed		179, 260
agreement		6, 110, 145, 197, 234-235
agreements		60, 80, 249
agrees 121
aiming 118, 198
alerts   100
aligned		23
Alignment		143
alleged		1
alliance		82
allocate		104
allocated		45, 52, 156
allowable		49
allowance		142
allowed		120, 171
allows 10, 168
almost 249
already		116, 157, 193, 221, 234
always 10
ambitious		236
amount		21, 160
amounts		232, 260
amplify 67, 111

269

analysis   3, 6, 10-11, 60, 64, 71-73, 87, 136, 140, 145, 172, 183, 189, 197, 205-206, 210-211, 214-215, 226, 236, 239, 247
analyze   2, 59, 62, 73
analyzed   100, 145, 150, 209
another   154, 163, 174
anothers   246
answer 11-12, 16, 28, 44, 59, 75, 91, 104, 224
answered   27, 43, 58, 74, 90, 103, 129
answering   11, 165, 253
anyone   28, 121, 124
anything   169, 173, 185, 228
appear   1
applicable   12, 91, 254, 263
applied   92, 140, 163, 251, 259
appointed   30, 41
approach   80, 105, 109, 160, 212, 222, 236, 245-246
approaches   77, 82, 199-200
approval   41, 108, 159
approvals   215
approved   34, 70, 140, 145, 148, 179, 186, 190, 223, 225, 260
approving   148
Architects   8
archives   261
arising 132
around 113, 115, 217
articulate   245-246
asking 1, 8, 191-192
aspects   165
assess 34, 80, 97, 120, 167, 206
assessed   82, 204
assessing   81, 95
assessment   5-6, 9-10, 18, 144-145, 195, 202, 205-206, 236-237, 239
assets 53
assign 22
assigned   142, 150, 154, 156-157, 177, 179-180, 193-194, 232, 241
assigning   171
assignment   5, 163, 193
assist   9, 63, 88, 98, 173, 184, 227
assistant   8
associated   230
assume   203-204

Assumption   3, 152
assurance   19, 142, 179, 198, 228
attainable   37, 196
attained   205
attempted   28
attempting   91
attend 26, 234
attendance   41
attendant   89
attended   41
attending   229
attention   12, 109
attitude   261
attitudes   222
attributes   4, 105, 146, 163, 223-224
auction   260
audited   261
auditing   24, 96, 119, 157
auditors   251-252
audits 215
author 1
authority   68, 145, 200, 202, 247, 264
authorize   223
authorized   140, 156-158, 262, 265
automatic   262
available   19, 30, 46, 69, 72, 77, 98, 120, 132, 156, 160, 162-163, 178, 187, 193, 201, 205, 207, 211, 230, 248, 252, 259
Average   12, 27, 43, 58, 74, 90, 103, 129, 253
background   10, 133, 165
backing   137
backward   225
balanced   86
balances   260
bandwidth   253
barriers 124, 242
Baseline   4, 159, 185
baselined   142, 198
baselines   32, 186
basics 108
because   178, 181
become   107, 112, 126-127, 145, 148, 205, 227
before 10, 28, 101, 162, 167, 175, 185, 202-203, 215, 223-224
beginning   2, 15, 27, 43, 58, 74, 90, 103, 129

behavior 245, 261
Behaviors 19, 227
behaviour 237, 259
belief 11, 16, 28, 44, 59, 75, 91, 104, 126
believable 115
believe 121, 126
benchmark 190
beneficial 190
benefit 1, 17, 25, 52, 93, 136, 173, 197
benefits 27, 45, 52, 61, 73, 104, 112, 114, 117-118, 139, 141, 152, 167, 205, 236, 264
besides 173
better 8, 51, 85, 162, 175-176, 184, 210, 220, 228, 232, 235, 255, 257, 265
between 68, 148, 153, 172-173, 215, 219, 224, 242, 257
beyond 246
biggest 55, 181
blinding 71
bother 53
bottleneck 175
bounce 66
boundaries 40, 234
bounds 40
Breakdown 3-4, 154, 171
briefed 30
brings 42
broken 62
brought 151
budget 95, 100, 120, 139, 157, 161, 179, 182, 186, 253-254, 256, 259
Budgeted 57, 156
budgets 18, 112, 156-158, 196, 247, 258
building 18, 94, 171, 249-250
burden 227
burn-in 255
business 1, 8, 10, 21-22, 34, 40, 52, 56-57, 69-70, 77, 86, 101, 107-108, 111-112, 114, 116, 118-119, 124, 128, 131, 133, 146, 153, 156-157, 211, 225, 252, 256-257, 264
busywork 139
buy-in 111, 255
Calculate 165
calculated 259
called 138

cannot 174
capability 239
capable 8, 29
capacities 126
capacity 18, 78, 139, 182, 240, 245
capital 126
capitalize 71, 245
capture 55, 94, 152, 261
captured 48, 70, 82, 123, 146, 159, 180, 223
career 148, 196
careers 114
carried 61, 210
categories 207
category 37, 157
caught 236
caused 1, 54
causes 44, 52, 55-56, 59, 65, 70, 101, 140
causing 20, 216
celebrate 77
celebrated 240
Center 1-7, 9-14, 16-27, 29-43, 45-103, 105-148, 150-157, 159-169, 171-187, 189, 191, 193, 195, 197-199, 201-209, 211-213, 215-217, 219-223, 225-227, 229, 232, 234, 236-237, 239, 241, 243-245, 247, 249-253, 255-259, 261, 263-266
centrally 86
challenge 8, 228
challenges 115, 131, 166, 219
chance 209
chances 205
change 6, 16, 23, 42, 45, 50, 65, 69-70, 74, 80, 84, 86, 100, 128, 134-135, 140, 144-145, 151, 154, 164, 178, 181, 185, 197, 203, 211-212, 217-218, 223-226, 242-243, 252, 261, 265
changed 26, 42, 93, 113, 120, 131, 147, 183, 202, 217
changes 25, 29, 34, 37, 56, 70, 81, 89, 99, 101, 113, 122-123, 140, 142, 151, 153, 156-158, 171, 174, 179, 186, 206, 217, 223-226, 232, 240, 262
changing 92, 115
channels 219, 243
chargeable 157
charged 156, 260
charges 259
charter 2, 38, 133-134, 138, 141
charting 215

charts 60
cheaper 51
checked 68, 93, 97-98
checklists 9, 160
choice 37, 124
choose 11
chosen 132, 209, 257
circumvent 22
claimed 1
claims 190
clarify 114
clearly 11, 16-17, 28, 32, 36, 39, 44, 59, 75, 79, 91, 104, 195, 202, 211
client 141, 210, 255
clients 19, 37, 229, 244, 251
closed 99, 193, 225, 261
closely 10, 178
Close-Out 7, 212, 261-263
closest 128
Closing 7, 61, 257
coaches 192
cognitive 239, 245
cognizant 240
coherently 230
colleague 123
colleagues 110, 113, 176
collect 60, 98, 183, 233
collected 42, 63, 65, 70, 73, 150
collecting 215
collection 72, 191, 266
combine 77
coming 64, 213
command 99
commit 237
commitment 194
committed 61, 207, 251
Committee 152, 216
common 197, 211, 213, 242
community 145, 175, 183-184, 203, 209
companies 1, 101
company 8, 51, 65, 107, 109, 111, 117, 123-124
compare 66, 75, 178, 250
compared 111, 197, 206

274

comparing   82
comparison   11, 247
compatible   225, 245-246
compelling   29
compete   239
competent   251
competitor   247
complaints   189, 260
complete   1, 9, 11, 18, 31-32, 36, 150, 161, 168, 172, 175-176, 179, 208, 234, 256, 262
completed   12, 30, 39, 150, 161, 167, 202, 215, 261
completely   127
completing   115, 155
completion   41-42, 150, 156-157, 179, 193-194, 230, 245, 250, 260, 263
complex   8, 110, 249
complexity   20, 47, 64, 224
compliance   24, 64, 80, 153, 187, 251
complied   233
component   187, 189
components   152-153, 178, 198, 212
compute   12
computing   127
concept   87
conceptual   219
concern   48, 82
concerned   21
concerns   19, 128, 253
concrete   82, 246
condition   92, 187
conditions   93, 105, 185, 233
conducted   213-214, 226
conference   213
confident   168
confirm   11
conflict145, 199, 234
conform   152
conjure   146
connected   178
connecting   128
consider   20, 22, 25, 163, 213
considered   16, 49, 189, 214, 227
considers   65

consistent	41, 49, 61, 96, 141, 152, 157, 194, 229, 248
Constraint	3, 152, 216
consultant	8, 181-182
consulted	127
consulting	49
consumers	112
contact	8, 160, 215
contacts	116
contain	20, 60, 99, 245
contained	1, 193
contains	9
content	38, 152, 227
contents	1-2, 9
context	29, 35-37
continual	97, 99
Continuity	56, 165
continuous	63
contract	7, 157, 159-160, 213, 221, 232-233, 248, 260-262
contractor	7, 247-248, 253, 265
contracts	41, 60, 136, 253, 261
contribute	147
control	2, 32, 57, 91-93, 96, 99-102, 144, 151, 156-157, 159, 174, 183, 193, 223-224, 227-228, 248, 260, 266
controlled	67
controls	20, 69, 76, 79-80, 92-94, 97-98, 101, 168, 204
convention	105
converge	245-246
conversion	153
convey	1
conveyed	265
convince	194
cooperate	183
copies	259
Copyright	1
correct	44, 91
corrective	101, 173
correspond	9-10
costing	50
counting	125, 161
counts	125
course	42, 50, 249
covering	9, 98, 196, 259
crashing	167

craziest 119
create 16, 105, 111, 151, 173, 189, 224, 240
created 64, 67, 93, 135, 138-139, 198, 244
creating 8, 55, 216
creative 20
creativity 76
credible 183
crisis 19
criteria 2, 5, 9-10, 34, 37, 59, 80, 84, 88, 95, 118, 130, 148, 150-151, 180, 183, 213, 261
CRITERION 2, 16, 28, 44, 59, 75, 91, 104
critical 37-38, 67, 83, 94, 96, 115, 143, 153, 165, 175, 180, 227, 240, 247
critically 193
criticism 64, 237
cross-sell 112
crucial 68, 165
crystal 12
culture 37, 62, 139, 142, 196, 240
current 42, 44, 47, 56, 66-68, 81, 100, 108, 111, 116, 120, 126, 143, 146, 152-153, 158, 174, 196-198, 211, 216, 224
currently 42, 121, 156, 248
custom 24
customer 18, 34-35, 42, 81, 97, 102, 104, 106, 123, 146, 185, 189, 201, 207-208, 224, 233, 247, 251-252, 256
customers 1, 26, 29, 48, 55, 66, 101, 104, 107, 109, 112-114, 116-117, 120, 123, 126, 146, 222, 233, 259
cut-down 249
damage 1, 205
Dashboard 9
dashboards 99
database 174
databases 191
day-to-day 97, 128, 166
deadlines 119, 165
dealing 20
decide 125, 196
deciding 125
decision 6, 57, 62, 77, 79-81, 83, 173, 203, 211, 227-228
decisions 75-76, 78-79, 81, 83-85, 95, 100, 159, 212, 220, 227, 232-233, 239
decrease 190
dedicated 8

deeper 11
defect 190
defects 189
Defender 1-7, 9-14, 16-27, 29-43, 45-103, 105-148, 150-157, 159-169, 171-187, 189, 191, 193, 195, 197-199, 201-209, 211-213, 215-217, 219-223, 225-227, 229, 232, 234, 236-237, 239, 241, 243-245, 247, 249-253, 255-259, 261, 263-266
define 2, 28, 35, 37, 39, 60, 68, 79, 154, 173, 206, 237
defined 11-12, 16-17, 20, 28-30, 32, 34-37, 39-42, 44, 59, 67, 75, 91, 104, 150, 154, 159, 163, 174, 177, 179-180, 198, 212, 216, 230
defines 21, 38, 40, 172
defining 8, 128
definite 99, 163
definition 17, 26, 31-32, 36, 40-41, 143, 185, 191, 265
degree 236-237, 239-240, 245-246
delayed 165
delaying 46
delays 51, 161, 176
delegated 29
delete 181
deletions 99
deliver 26, 37, 81, 114, 122, 176, 184, 233-234
delivered 50, 118, 185, 257, 263, 265
delivery 45, 105, 168, 217, 261
demand 123
demands 245
department 8, 111, 222, 247
depend 221
dependent 258
depends 109
depict 168
deploy 101, 116
deployed 94
deploying 49
deployment 57
derive 95
describe 21, 145, 148, 152, 253-254, 265
described 1, 160, 202, 225
deserving 221
design 1, 10, 62, 76, 86, 99, 109, 138-139, 215, 248
designated 159
designed 8, 10, 72, 84, 89

designing	8
desired 19, 30, 65, 84, 172, 185, 250, 263
detail 88, 155, 264
detailed	67, 73, 139, 157, 211
details 51
detect 93
determine	10, 108, 119, 138, 161-162, 183, 206, 234, 259
determined	71, 109, 191-192
detracting	119
develop	44, 75, 78, 86, 140-141, 144-145, 154, 182, 204, 238
developed	10, 38-40, 52, 88, 144, 151, 191, 225, 239, 249
developers	206
developing	71, 83, 214, 218
devices	230
diagram	4, 50, 57, 59, 140, 167-168
diagrams	53, 215
dictates	178
Dictionary	3, 156
difference	151, 172-173, 219, 227
different	8, 22, 29, 35, 38, 59, 63, 108-109, 139, 195, 198, 216, 219
difficult 63, 164, 167, 171, 186
difficulty	219
dilemma	115
dimensions	24
direct 156-157, 239
direction	42, 51, 140
directions	209
directly 1, 66, 136, 157
Directory	6, 232
Disagree	11, 16, 28, 44, 59, 75, 91, 104
disaster	54, 56
disclosure	101
discover	144
discussion	127
display 165
displayed	69, 162, 175
disposed	229
disputes	262
disqualify	61
disruptive	69
distribute	173, 232

divide 235
Divided 27, 29, 43, 57, 74, 90, 103, 129
document 10, 146, 150, 153, 159, 227, 233, 265
documented 33, 79, 87, 96-97, 100, 132, 150, 153, 160, 186, 195, 256, 265
documents 8, 153, 157, 178, 235, 240, 260
domains 78
dormant 116
drawbacks 193
drawing 207
Driver 68
drivers 45, 70
drives 50
driving 104, 107
duplicates 145
Duration 4, 154, 173, 175, 212
durations 34
during 42, 89, 131-132, 152, 160, 164, 169, 190, 193, 201, 205, 207, 213, 217, 230, 265-266
dynamics 37
earlier 120
earned 7, 174, 249-250
easily 151, 174
economic 209
economical 106
economy 83, 174
eDiscovery 228
edition 9
editorial 1
educate 257
education 17, 96
effect 139, 203, 205-206, 257
effective 21, 25, 106, 112, 127, 147, 152, 228-231, 265-266
effects 53, 137-138, 165
efficiency 69, 92, 174
efficient 45, 80, 222, 266
effort 36, 46, 54, 127, 144, 157, 194, 212, 242
efforts 28, 87, 187, 215, 258
either 163
electronic 1, 260
element 157
elements 10, 40, 64, 99, 108-109, 157, 191, 194, 232, 240
Elevator 147

elicit 191
eliminate 209
eliminated 187
embarking 29
emerging 65, 97
emphasis 228
employee 125, 253
employees 19-20, 64, 106, 110, 123, 230, 240, 259
employers 135
empower 8
enable 69
enablers 107
encourage 76, 102, 237
endure 182
end-users 260
engage 107, 237, 246
engagement 55, 135, 200
enhance 93, 245, 252
enhanced 114
enhancing 102
enlarged 207
enough 8, 70, 109-110, 120, 142, 148, 180, 207
ensure 34, 39, 60, 89, 106, 110, 112, 122, 138, 182, 188, 192, 196, 214, 244, 252
ensures 122
ensuring 10, 249
Enterprise 222
entire 248
entities 56
entity 1
equally 260
equipment 22, 131, 251
equitably 29, 235
equivalent 180
errors 112
escalated 220, 257
essential 83
establish 75, 101, 183
estimate 47, 49, 52, 151, 175-176, 181, 256
estimated 41-42, 49, 56, 108, 140, 179, 181, 183-184, 204, 253-254
estimates 4, 42, 54, 68, 143, 156, 173, 181, 194, 211, 215
estimating 4, 159, 175, 181, 183, 211

estimation 78, 212
estimators 181
etcetera 47, 105
ethical 24, 117, 243, 255
ethnic 111
evaluate 76, 85, 88, 137, 156, 173, 214
evaluated 132, 186
evaluating 84, 88
evaluation 59, 79, 84, 99, 214, 243, 246
evaluative 219
evaluators 214
events 26, 78, 80, 84, 157
everyday 64
everyone 29, 37
everything 53, 228
evidence 11, 49, 190, 222, 230, 251, 260
evident 215
evolution 44
evolve 100
examined 34
example 2, 9, 13, 66, 101, 140, 153, 157, 236
examples 8-9, 133
exceed 154
exceeding 55, 196
excellence 8, 40
excellent 55
excelling 196
except 260
excessive 159
exclude 81
execute 256
executed 226
executing 6, 187, 199, 207, 219
execution 101, 131, 223, 232
executive 8, 106
executives 115
exercise 23
exercises 237
exerted 263
existing 10, 101, 120, 134, 151, 266
expect 126, 145, 175, 179, 214, 264
expected 27, 34, 82, 110, 123, 140, 182, 228, 243, 247, 263
expenses 235

experience   105, 109, 128, 165, 176, 208, 253
experiment   114
expertise   77, 198, 234
experts 31
explained   10
explicit 191
explicitly   122
explore   59, 206, 236
export 136
exposures   82
extend 239
extent 11, 17, 20-21, 31, 88, 138, 248
external   28, 106, 180, 194, 205
facilitate   11, 72, 99, 245
facilities   147, 213, 230
facility 251
facing 22, 115
factors 54, 80, 119, 184, 240, 243
failed 47
failure 54, 119, 122, 152, 173, 209, 258
fairly   29
familiar 9
fashion 1
feasible   52, 65, 117, 183
feature 10
features   140, 255
feedback   35, 42, 47, 132, 235
finalize 212
finalized   13
financial   53, 68-69, 73, 106, 121, 137, 139
findings   190
fingertips   10
finish   162-163, 166, 168, 175, 250
fitness 252
flowery 145
follow 96, 107, 121, 167, 235
followed   42, 159, 223
following   9, 11
for--and   95
forecast   179, 249
Forecasts   179
forefront   116
foresee   166

283

foreseen 132
forever 113
forget 10
formal 7, 110, 143, 145, 159, 201, 245, 255-256
formally 34, 185, 194, 207, 251
format 10, 232
formats 201
formed 240
formula 12, 114
Formulate 28
forward 107
foster 105, 114
framework 99, 125, 191-192
freaky 120
frequency 34, 96, 119, 191, 209, 229
frequent 159
frequently 56, 136, 236
friend 112, 115, 123
frontiers 80
fulfill 109
full-blown 46
full-scale 86
function 198, 244, 255, 259-260, 265
functional 157, 180, 235
functions 35, 60, 123, 126, 146, 171, 174, 179, 232, 245
funded 257
funding 106, 110, 131
further 203
future 8, 48, 94, 99, 127, 205, 239, 247
gained 73, 100, 102
garbage 229
gather 11, 30-31, 33, 35-36, 39, 44, 61, 72
gathered 38, 61-62, 66, 70, 72, 145
gathering 32-33, 38
general 78, 163, 174, 197, 256
generally 222
generate 65, 72, 190
generated 73, 131, 194
generation 9
geographic 234
getting 53, 142, 227
global 83, 127, 166
govern 109

governance   25, 120, 195, 240
governing   200
government   265
graded   203
granted   239
graphics   22
graphs 9
greater   140
ground 73
grouped   163
groups 109, 142, 152, 171, 221
growth 71, 118
guarantee   81
guidance   1, 190
guidelines   213, 227
guiding   136, 230
handle 170, 207, 210, 232
handled   235
happen   24, 203, 209-210, 218, 224
happened   224
happening   128, 210
happens   8, 29, 50, 110, 119, 142, 184, 189, 203-204, 209-210, 229, 262
hardest   49
hardly 250
hardware   201, 220
Havent 114, 202
Having 203
headed   197
health 124, 229
hearing   111
helpful 173, 193
helping   8
hidden 54
higher 190
high-level   30, 146
Highly 69
high-tech   127
hijacking   108
hiring 98
historical   183
history 161, 181, 266
hitters 60

hitting 249
holidays 142
honest 117
horizon 125
humans 8
hypotheses 59
identified 1, 18-19, 22-23, 34, 61, 68, 73, 87, 131-132, 142-143, 153, 156, 160, 179, 186, 193-195, 212, 227, 232, 241, 247, 257
identify 10-11, 21, 23, 65, 71, 82, 136, 151, 183, 194, 230
identity 237
ignore 26
ignoring 115
images 146
imbedded 102
immediate 137, 204
impact 5, 29, 47-48, 52, 54-57, 86, 126, 139, 147, 179, 186, 203-205, 207-208, 225-226, 232, 237, 243
impacted 47, 152-153, 263
impacts 49, 52, 152, 175, 204, 264
Implement 18, 91
implicit 126
import 136
importance 236
important 18, 26, 41, 66-67, 105, 117-118, 121, 138, 172, 190, 200, 217, 219
improve 2, 10-11, 68, 75-77, 79-87, 89-90, 181, 188, 190, 232, 257
improved 77, 81-82, 86, 92, 263
improves 131
improving 89, 222
inactive 181
incentives 99
include 22, 77, 81, 159-161, 197, 211, 213, 247
included 2, 8, 21, 53, 139, 146, 176, 183, 189, 201, 207, 215, 223, 253-254, 261
INCLUDES 10
including 37, 49, 53, 69, 94, 98-99, 153, 239, 241
increase 88, 117, 174, 248
increased 124, 195
increasing 105, 228
incurred 55
incurring 156
in-depth 9, 11

286

indicate 61, 92, 118
indicated 101
indicators 18, 55-56, 66, 73, 81, 94, 187
indirect 156, 239, 247
indirectly 1
individual 1, 46, 131, 175, 177, 198, 235, 246, 260
induction 251
industries 205
industry 93, 111, 121, 252
infinite 127
influence 80, 106, 135, 199, 212, 227-228, 263
influences 166
informal 245-246
informed 117
ingrained 102
inherent 120
initial 39, 125, 178, 260
initially 38
initiated 183, 189, 226
Initiating 2, 122, 131
initiative 11, 192, 199, 241
Innovate 75
innovation 56, 62, 69, 83, 99, 109, 114
innovative 105, 176, 184, 219
inputs 35, 54, 69, 94, 143, 174
inside 19
insight 72
insights 9
inspect 223
inspector 223
inspired 122
Instead 116
instructed 144
integrate 89, 98, 128
integrated 132, 186, 252
integrity 127, 225
intended 1
INTENT 16, 28, 44, 59, 75, 91, 104
intention 1
interact 123
interest 111, 221
interests 21
interface 201

interfaces   153
intergroup   237
interim 119
internal   1, 28, 63, 106, 157-158, 260
interpret   11
interval 193
interview   117
introduced   245
invalid 159
inventory   182
invest 66
investment   21, 47, 65, 187, 207
investor   44
invoice 232
involve 122, 136, 142
involved   21, 26, 29, 60, 62, 71, 83, 128, 143-144, 152, 159, 195-196, 211, 218, 222, 236, 243, 251, 259, 261, 264
involves   95
issued 190
issues   19-20, 23-26, 147, 150-152, 169, 189, 212, 220, 232, 241, 257
iteration   179
itself   1, 19
jointly   236
judgment   1
justified 101, 266
killer   105
knowledge   10, 28, 36, 73, 77, 81, 93, 97, 99-100, 102, 105, 119, 124, 196, 261
lacked 93
largely 67
latest 9
laundry   145
leader 25, 62, 81, 207, 234, 239
leaders 37, 60, 66, 116, 128
leadership   23, 33, 39, 83, 116, 124, 151, 234
learned   7, 94, 123, 191, 255, 257, 264-265
learning   93, 99, 142, 228-229, 239
ledger 174
lesson   257, 263, 265
lessons 7, 86, 94, 123, 191, 255, 265
levels   41, 66, 81, 93, 99, 124, 136, 193, 247
leverage   40, 83, 94, 128, 175, 184

leveraged 28
liability 1
licensed 1
lifecycle 47, 74
lifecycles 77
Lifetime 10
likelihood 77, 205, 210
likely 80, 100, 123, 186, 205, 213, 228, 230
limitation 51
limited 10
Linked 33, 227
listed 1, 177, 191, 197
listen 107, 113, 234
little 145
locally 86, 197
located 197, 230
locations 188
logged 224
logical 168-169, 248
longer 99
long-term 96, 116
looking 26, 182
losing 48
losses 24, 39
lowest 168
magnitude 77
maintain 91, 118, 127
maintained 156, 245
makers 77, 97, 211
making 25, 62, 79-81, 128, 192, 203, 239
manage 33-35, 49, 54, 68, 76-77, 81, 85, 117, 124, 134, 136, 141, 148, 153, 166, 177, 185, 187, 233, 241
manageable 31, 212
managed 8, 32, 64, 71, 74, 78, 86, 89, 96, 100, 150, 174, 206
management 1, 3-6, 9-10, 18, 21, 25, 46, 62-65, 70-71, 81, 83, 85-86, 88-89, 124, 128, 138-144, 150-151, 153, 156, 159, 163, 171, 173-174, 177-179, 181, 185-187, 190, 195, 197, 199, 201-203, 211-213, 215-218, 220, 222, 227, 232, 243, 247, 250, 252, 255, 260-261, 263, 265
manager 8, 10, 19, 39, 41, 119, 133, 141, 143, 151, 174, 212, 222, 255
managers 2, 130, 141, 193, 207, 251
manages 85, 88, 253

managing 2, 87, 130, 135-136, 216, 252
mandatory 225, 263
manner 24, 85, 152, 157, 194, 220, 245, 248, 255, 260
manpower 157
mantle 116
manual 187
mapping 64, 71
marked 150
market 20, 174, 204, 247, 249
marketable 204
marketer 8
Marketing 112
markets 22
material 133, 157, 194, 213
materials 1
matrices 148
Matrix 3, 5, 136, 148-149, 173, 193, 207
matter 31, 55-56, 237, 251
mattered 266
maximizing 125, 173
meaning 164
meaningful 57, 128, 245
measurable 35, 37, 132
measure 2, 10, 21, 24, 32, 40, 44-47, 49, 51-52, 54, 56-57, 64, 69, 75-76, 79, 86, 88, 91-92, 94, 98, 136-137, 183, 188-190, 219, 237
measured 25, 47-54, 56, 84, 94, 102, 210, 236-237
measures 46, 53, 55-56, 63, 66, 69, 81, 92-94, 187, 191, 209, 219
measuring 102, 247
mechanical 1
mechanism 152, 252
medium 237, 249
meeting 32-33, 97, 160, 186, 192, 196, 222, 227, 232, 234
meetings 28, 32, 41, 150, 193, 211, 227, 234-235, 266
member 6, 33, 107, 124, 142, 221, 235, 239
members 29, 98, 143, 159, 193, 197, 200, 211, 214, 233-237, 241, 245-246, 259
membership 246
memorable 245
mentors 201
message 98, 217
messages 234

method   46, 140, 151, 163, 199, 217, 237, 251
methods   34-35, 52, 72, 140, 179, 183, 188, 234
metrics 4, 42, 68, 99, 144, 189-190, 212
milestone   4, 165, 168, 197
milestones   135, 159, 163, 167
minimal   237
minimize   139, 243
minimizing   74, 125
minimum   253
minority   21
minutes   33, 83, 232
missed 50, 111
missing 69, 111, 163, 266
mission 65, 67, 117, 123, 196, 209, 245
mitigate   84, 151, 243
mitigated   257
mitigation   140, 212
mix-ups   230
modeling   67
models 20, 53, 72, 115
modern   212
modified   101, 223
modifier   189
moment   118
moments   68
momentum   109, 111
monetary   25, 243
monitor   91, 95, 98, 100, 183, 244, 259
monitored   95-96, 100, 132, 161, 259
monitoring   6, 92, 97, 100-102, 144, 169, 206, 215, 243, 260
months 83
motivate   111, 245
motivation   17, 100, 133, 136
motive 191-192
multiple   229, 251
narrative   165
narrow 69
national   209
nearest   12
nearly 121
necessary   62, 65, 67, 72, 85, 105, 115, 122, 138-139, 183,
193, 202, 225, 232, 244, 260

needed 16-18, 24-27, 35, 67, 69, 97, 99, 101, 133, 143, 175, 211, 220
negative 116, 177
negatively 263
negotiate 259
negotiated 110
neither 1
network 4, 167-168, 246
Neutral 11, 16, 28, 44, 59, 75, 91, 104
nominal 260
normal 102, 189
normalized 214
Notice 1
notified 199, 261
notifies 189
noting 223
number 27, 43, 55, 57, 74, 90, 103, 129, 171, 251, 268
numbers 108
numerous 262
objection 22, 25
objective 8, 49, 131, 133, 136-137, 151, 186, 227, 248
objectives 18, 22-23, 28, 33-34, 65, 67, 95, 98, 112, 118, 121-122, 138, 143, 147, 152, 160, 179, 204, 222, 233, 239, 242, 263
observed 76
obstacles 22, 176, 184
obtain 113, 264
obtained 42
obtaining 54
obvious 236
obviously 11
occurring 81, 132, 203, 208
occurs 19, 54, 101, 131, 207, 219
offerings 66, 75
office 213, 216, 222, 261
officials 262
one-time 8
ongoing 83, 94, 161
on-site 233
opened 193
operate 209, 234
operates 121
operating 6, 53, 57, 96, 156, 185, 224, 234-235
operation 93, 185

operations	10, 98, 102, 185
operators	96, 251
opinion	229
opinions	206
opponent	228
opposite	121, 126
opposition	105
optimal	213, 253
optimize	80, 102
optimized	117
option	124
options	19, 181, 239
orders	260
orient	97
oriented	160
origin	266
original	158, 178, 202, 227
originally	198, 216
originate	97, 200
others	145, 178, 183, 196, 199, 204, 207, 237-238, 257
otherwise	1
outcome	11, 81, 136, 172, 232
outcomes	85, 102, 122, 176, 184, 229, 250, 263
outlier	163
outlined	95
output	40, 59-60, 64-65, 68, 73, 92-93, 150
outputs	61-63, 68-69, 72, 94, 137, 169, 174
outside	76, 131, 211
Outsource	61, 134
outweigh	52, 205
overall	11, 23, 57, 98, 111, 124, 147, 167, 206, 219, 228, 244, 253
overcome	176, 184
overhead	156, 193-194, 247-248, 266
overheads	179
overlooked	220, 257
oversees	131
oversight	152, 216
overtime	164
owners	154
ownership	32, 97
package	156-157, 247
packages	194
paradigms	108

paragraph   110
parameters   96, 188
Pareto 60, 215
particular   66
Parties 82, 141, 261-262
partners   26, 29, 82, 102, 109, 116, 123, 136, 139, 236, 264
pattern   163
patterns   78
paycheck   124
paying 109
payment   137, 215, 260-261
payments   160
pending   225
people 8, 22, 54-55, 63-64, 79, 83, 95, 102, 105, 107, 114, 116, 118-119, 123, 126-128, 187, 192-194, 205, 207, 209, 216-217, 221, 234, 249, 251
perceive   117
perceived   236
percent   120
percentage   148
perception   86-87, 117
perform   22, 29, 40, 145, 152, 161, 171, 205, 255
performed   83, 148, 156, 161-162, 203, 248
performing   194, 213, 220
perhaps   26, 249
period 89, 156, 248
periodic   212
permission   1
person 1, 26, 165, 193, 199
personal   106
personally   148
personnel   25-26, 62, 100, 142, 180, 192, 198, 229, 265
pertaining   131, 205
pertinent   100
phases 47, 163
pitfalls 120
placements   229
places 213
planet 95
planned   95-96, 98, 101, 132, 169, 204, 220, 248, 263
planners   97
planning   3, 9, 98, 101, 131, 138-139, 141, 143-144, 157, 169, 171, 221, 230, 243, 247

platforms	239
players	78
please	214
pocket	184
pockets	184
points	27, 43, 57, 73-74, 90, 102-103, 129, 191
policies	205, 217, 252, 259
policy	34, 79, 97, 153, 169, 259
Political	36, 121, 165
portfolio	121, 243
portfolios	241
portion	178
portray	60
position	196
positioned	183-184
positions	230
positive	111, 116, 140, 153, 199, 229, 237
positively	263
possess	239
possible	47, 57, 65, 69, 84, 91, 124, 127, 142, 206, 230
possibly	208
potential	16, 54, 61, 81, 85, 88, 108, 126, 157, 204-205, 234, 242-243
practical	65, 75, 78, 91, 221
practiced	132
practices	1, 10, 74, 78, 94, 98, 141, 212, 217, 255
precaution	1
precede	168
predict	223
predicting	102
predictive	172
predictor	171
preferred	217
pre-filled	9
prepare	173, 191, 195, 200
prepared	213
preparing	178, 260
present	99, 119, 127, 187, 198, 219, 251
presented	17, 223, 233
preserve	41
preserved	72
pressures	165
prevent	46, 142, 157, 159, 229

prevented 230
preventive 209
prevents 25
previous 28, 131, 190, 253
previously 140, 225, 259
priced 157
prices 259-260
primary 53, 133, 172
principles 212, 239
priorities 45-46
priority 53-54
privacy 32
problem 16-17, 19-20, 24, 26, 28, 31, 37, 45, 65, 73, 207, 221, 228, 249
problems 17-18, 20, 22-23, 78, 81, 101, 113, 146, 150, 191, 243
procedural 239
procedure 230
procedures 10, 87, 96-97, 143, 153, 157, 169, 174, 187-188, 217, 223, 228, 235, 247
proceeding 175, 178
process 1-3, 5-8, 10, 30, 35, 38, 40, 42, 47, 60, 62-74, 76, 92-94, 96-97, 99-100, 102, 131-132, 138-139, 144, 146, 148, 150-151, 153, 159, 169, 187-188, 191-192, 201, 206, 211, 215, 219, 227, 232-233, 236, 243, 248-249, 252-253, 255, 257, 265-266
processes 56-57, 59-63, 67-69, 71-72, 98-99, 101, 131-132, 153, 201, 206, 212, 217, 225, 251, 255, 257, 266
produce 68, 134, 169, 221
produced 64, 139
produces 163
producing 148, 150
product 1, 49, 66, 105, 123, 151, 185-186, 190, 204, 208, 210, 221, 225, 232, 241, 249-251, 256-257, 263, 265-266
production 29, 83, 124
products 1, 17, 55, 107, 122, 134, 139, 148, 185, 201, 220, 222, 243-244, 246
profit 190
profits 186
program 19, 63, 95, 131, 139, 141, 181, 196, 201, 219, 230, 244
programme 139
programs 221, 241

progress   30, 52, 76, 98, 106, 128, 137, 183, 187, 192, 197, 237, 243-244
project 2-4, 6-9, 20-22, 24, 39, 46, 60, 66, 74, 95-96, 106, 108, 110, 118-119, 121-122, 126, 130-148, 150-155, 159-168, 171-186, 189, 195, 197-199, 201-208, 211-212, 215-216, 219-222, 225-226, 232, 237, 241, 243-245, 249-253, 255-258, 261, 263-266
projected   156-157, 193, 247
projection   160, 208
projects   2, 46, 120, 130-131, 136, 138-139, 148, 150, 153-154, 174, 182, 187, 202, 206, 221-222, 241, 249-251, 258
promising   105
promote   55, 64
promotion   195
promotions   142
promptly   220, 257
proofing   76
proper 101, 215, 251
properly   30, 37, 132, 146, 223, 260
proposal   165
proposals   97, 173, 213
proposed   18, 47, 56, 84, 140, 146-147, 198, 253
Propriety   243
protect   119
protected   72
protection   125, 201
proved 255
provide   19, 72, 106, 108, 110, 135, 146, 157, 174, 176, 178, 184, 193, 216, 243, 246
provided   12, 94, 142, 159, 198, 214
providers   82
provides   165, 171
providing   101, 135, 165, 185
provision   227
provokes   218
public 139
publisher   1
pulled 120
purchase   8, 213, 260
purpose   2, 10, 123, 136, 171-172, 177, 183, 191, 224, 227, 236-237, 245
pushing   121
qualified   29, 67, 69, 72-73, 151, 251
qualifies   67, 72

qualify 49, 63, 66
qualifying   178
qualities   26, 239
quality 1, 4, 6, 10, 19, 53-54, 56, 60, 62-63, 68, 89, 92-93, 114, 138-139, 142, 174, 177-179, 187-189, 192, 196-198, 206, 212, 215, 228-232, 244
quantified   92
quantify   49
quantities   213
question   11-12, 16, 28, 44, 59, 75, 91, 104, 116, 136, 191
questions   8-9, 11, 65, 219
quickly 10, 66, 202
radically   69
raised 150
raising 138
raters   240
rather   117
rating   180
rational   157, 194
rationale   211, 228
reached   26
reaching   112
reaction   208
reactivate   116
readiness   29
readings   98, 139
realism 214
realistic   26, 60, 119, 207, 219, 239
realize 45
realized   112, 256
really   8, 20, 31, 143
reason 113, 126
reasonable   123, 143, 211, 215, 259
reasons   29
re-assign   163
rebuild 105
recast 182
receipt 230, 260
receive   9-10, 41, 47, 137, 213
received   30, 118, 202, 237, 266
recently   106
recipient   17, 262
recognised   80

298

recognize   2, 16, 19-21, 25, 77-78, 88
recognized   16-19, 21, 23-24, 70, 241, 245, 259
recognizes   19
recommend   115, 123, 199
record 234
recording   1, 223, 234
records   69, 111, 156-157, 261
recovery   56, 152
recruiting   230
redefine   26, 37
re-design   62
reduce 48, 54, 204, 227
reducing   97, 105
references   268
reflect 73, 95, 98, 215
reform 56, 97, 113, 117
reforms 18, 47, 52
refuse 229
refuses 210
regarding   106, 127, 213-214, 222
Register   2, 5, 135, 145, 203-204, 207
regret 79
regular 30, 32, 70, 253
regularly   41, 186, 211
regulated   224
regulatory   24, 232
reimbursed   235
rejected   223
relate 71, 173, 225
related 20, 49, 61, 96, 131, 150, 185, 193, 223-224, 241, 250, 265
relating   185
relation   21-22, 84, 123, 229
relations   106
relative 98, 187, 236
relatively   110
release 179, 190
released   224
releases   254
relevant   37, 56, 72, 99, 113, 215, 229, 232, 239, 246
reliable 209
reliably 237
remain 37
remaining   184

299

remove 209
remunerate 125
repair 230
repeat 131
rephrased 10
replace 51
replanning 158
replicated 257
Report 6-7, 82, 98, 165, 189, 221, 230, 245, 253
reported 156, 241, 249
reporting 97, 124, 158, 194, 201, 223, 252
reports 47, 98, 135, 141, 159
repository 197, 211
represent 84, 185, 225
reproduced 1
reputation 121
request 6, 65, 145, 185, 197, 211, 223-226
requested 1, 81, 223, 226
requests 213, 223-224
require 31, 46, 73, 101, 169
required 23, 29-30, 32, 36, 42, 51, 61-62, 86-87, 93, 132, 146, 161-163, 176, 178, 191, 201, 203, 215, 243, 252, 260, 264, 266
requires 131
requiring 135, 262
research 20, 105, 121
Reserve 181
reserved 1
reserves 156, 160
reside 84, 197, 211
resolution 72, 78, 199
resolve 23, 26, 163
resolved 220, 257
resource 4-5, 120, 143, 157, 163, 169, 171-172, 174, 197, 211, 221
resources 2, 8, 22, 25, 27, 30, 48, 65, 87, 93-94, 104, 120, 127, 131-132, 136, 143, 162-163, 175, 184, 198, 215, 241, 243, 246, 251
respect 1
respond 139, 203
responded 12
response 19-20, 92, 94, 99, 101-102, 253
responses 77, 116, 203, 214
responsive 183

result   61, 84, 151, 182-183, 189, 226, 262, 264
resulted   97
resulting   73, 138, 140, 158
results 9, 34, 37, 66, 75, 77, 79, 82-83, 85, 88, 94, 138, 142, 182, 184, 187, 189-191, 243, 248, 256
Retain 104
retained   70
retention   54
retrospect   120
return   106, 167, 187
returns 189
revenue   24, 51
revenues   53
review 10, 29, 62, 168, 177, 187, 193, 197, 215, 230
reviewed   40, 132, 260
reviewers   237
reviews 142, 167, 201, 208, 215, 239, 248
revised 68, 97
revisions   262
reward 46, 55, 63, 221
rewards   99
rework 50, 55
rights   1
roadblocks   142
robustness   165
routine 95
rubbish 230
safely   210, 252
safety   122
samples   188
sampling   215
satisfied   111, 233, 255-256
satisfies 249
satisfying   107
savings 42, 45, 50, 68
scalable   83
scenario   36, 39, 219
schedule   3-4, 42, 51, 100, 108, 140, 144, 159, 167, 177-180, 186, 197, 202-204, 211-212, 215, 220, 225, 232, 248, 254
scheduled   211
schedules   157, 177
scheduling   194, 211
scheme   99

301

science 70
scopes 151
Scorecard 2, 12-14
scorecards 99
Scores 14
scoring 10
Screen 223
screening 190, 252, 260
scripts 152
second 12
section 12, 27, 43, 57-58, 74, 90, 102-103, 129
sections 153
sector 249
securing 55, 108
Security 1-7, 9-14, 16-27, 29-43, 45-103, 105-148, 150-157, 159-169, 171-187, 189, 191, 193, 195, 197-199, 201-209, 211-213, 215-217, 219-223, 225-227, 229, 232, 234, 236-237, 239, 241, 243-245, 247, 249-253, 255-259, 261, 263-266
segments 29, 109
select 62, 98
selected 78, 183, 206
selecting 73
selection 5, 173, 213-214, 260
seller 213
sellers 1
selling 104
senior 116, 124, 236
sensitive 35, 48
sequence 168
sequencing 117, 138, 143
series 11
service 1-2, 8, 49, 82, 86-87, 93, 105, 151, 185, 204, 213, 221, 266
services 1, 31, 45, 49, 55, 106-107, 112, 234, 253-255, 262
session 144
setbacks 66
setting 118-119
several 63
severely 62
severity 204
shared 100, 184, 227, 234
sharing 81, 93, 142
shifts 20

should 8, 24, 26, 31, 38, 47, 53, 55, 62, 66, 70-71, 73, 75-76, 84, 87, 92, 96, 105, 107, 110, 120, 124-125, 135, 138-140, 156, 161, 163, 165, 173, 181, 189, 191, 195-196, 204-207, 213-214, 217-218, 224, 226, 232, 240, 243, 247
signature 112
signatures 169
signers 262
similar 28, 39, 60, 66, 75, 161, 190, 199
simple 110, 249
simply 9, 227
simulator 237
single 110, 157, 234
single-use 8
situation 18, 44, 131, 203, 249, 257
situations 93
skeptical 113
skills 22, 61, 105, 119, 132, 160, 165, 207, 215, 220, 238, 244-246, 252, 266
slippage 205
smallest 24
social 113, 209, 237
societal 109
software 132, 173-174, 201-202, 207, 212, 214, 220, 224, 251-252, 254
solicit 35, 235
solution 57, 65, 72, 75, 78, 81, 83-86, 88-89, 91, 152, 209, 253
solutions 46, 79-80, 82, 85, 88, 94, 206, 265
solved 24
someone 8, 260
something 121, 140
Sometimes 46
sought 136
source 5, 106, 113, 173, 209, 211, 213-214
sources 30, 59-60, 205, 234
special 36, 94
specific 9, 19, 34-35, 37, 65, 107, 131, 153, 164, 167, 170-171, 177, 186, 205, 221, 225, 237, 251, 257
specified 112, 158, 194, 209, 257, 263, 265
specify 246
Speech 147
spoken 106
sponsor 18, 141-142, 211, 219, 256

sponsors   26, 211, 233, 236
spread 92, 98
stable 202
staffed 30
staffing 98, 141
staffs   239
stages 141, 230
standard   8, 93, 100, 132, 169, 251, 253-254
standards   1, 10-11, 91-92, 99, 102, 152, 189, 192, 214, 225
started 9
starting 10
starts   139
startup 133
start-up   233
stated 122, 157, 193, 234
Statement   3, 11, 78, 133, 142, 150, 153, 160, 182, 198
statements   12, 27, 37, 43, 58, 73-74, 90, 103, 129, 145, 151, 191, 229
static   223
statistics   150
status 6-7, 64, 159, 194, 197, 202, 206, 221, 224, 241, 249-250, 253
statutory   232
steady 48
Steering   152, 216
storage   230
stored 229
stories 36
strategic   45, 88, 98, 121, 143, 251
strategies   88, 99, 105, 113, 138, 212, 217, 227-228, 239, 266
strategy   23, 35, 48, 86, 88, 94, 104, 111, 114, 120, 138-139, 182, 187, 218, 228, 263, 266
Stream 64
strengths   165, 186, 235, 255
stretch 118
strict   70
strictly 260
strive   118
Strongly   11, 16, 28, 44, 59, 75, 91, 104, 224
structure   3-4, 51, 110, 120, 150, 154, 171, 177, 213, 230
structured   119, 212
structures   139
stupid 125

subdivide 157
subfactor 214
subject 9-10, 31
Subjective 145, 189
subjects 69
submitted 225-226
submitting 189
subset 24
succeed 56, 109, 237
success 21, 23, 29, 31-32, 36, 42, 44, 52, 54, 57, 77, 79, 81, 88, 102, 105-106, 108, 112, 114, 118-119, 122, 151, 173, 180-181, 205, 219, 221
successes 106
successful 71, 88-89, 93, 105, 118, 172, 186, 199, 221, 239
succession 93
suddenly 207
suffered 237
sufficient 139, 229-230, 259-260
suggested 101, 185, 225
supplier 85, 123
suppliers 61, 67, 116, 198, 259-260
supplies 256
supply 48, 165
support 8, 22, 61, 85, 93-94, 102, 105-106, 146, 157, 170, 196, 207, 251, 253
supported 60, 147
supporting 101, 143, 191
supportive 196, 212
supports 131
surface 101
SUSTAIN 2, 80, 104
sustained 182
sustaining 96
symptom 16, 53
system 10, 33, 65, 73, 99, 116, 128, 146-147, 157, 171, 187, 194-195, 215, 225, 229-230, 247, 249
systematic 45, 248
systems 63, 69, 71-72, 81, 98, 120, 142, 153, 180, 187, 217, 219, 230, 250, 256, 260
tackle 53
tactics 227-228
takers 150
taking 51, 173, 222

talent 72, 124
talents 105
talking 8
target 41
targeted   239
targets 118, 132, 249
tasked 97
teaching   231
technical   77, 131, 153, 166, 180, 201, 265
techniques   72, 115
technology   51, 86, 93, 105, 201, 208, 234
templates   8-9
tender 260
tenderers   260
testable   30
tested 19, 188
testing 88, 188, 190
themes 245
themselves   126, 237
theories   173
theory 100
therefore   210
therein 193
theyre 145
things 80, 116, 181, 257-258, 266
thinking   71, 76, 109
third- 82
thorough   77, 226
thoroughly   150
thought   234
threat 19, 109
threats 142
through   62, 70, 116, 230, 236
throughout   1, 74, 127, 152, 167
throughput   173
tighter 112
time-bound   37
timeframe   163, 183
timeframes   23
timeline   225, 244
timely 24, 85, 194, 220, 230, 232
Timescales   165
timetable   167

timing 207
together   105, 235, 239
toilet   230
tolerances   88
tolerated   161
tomorrow   95, 124
top-down   99
topics 77
touched   146
toward 97, 222
towards   72, 139
traced 152, 185
tracked   174, 197
tracking   33, 98, 144, 151, 177, 187
traction   113
trademark   1
trademarks   1
trained 37, 214
training   18, 22-23, 25, 60, 62, 76, 94, 96, 98, 142, 196, 198, 202, 215, 217, 222, 239, 259
trainings   24
Transfer   12, 27, 43, 58, 74, 90, 97, 99, 103, 129, 253
transition   145
translated   35
travel 259
trending   215
trends 65-66, 81, 117, 140, 150, 187, 209
trigger 79, 88
triggers 82, 159
triple   216
trophy 116
trouble 122
trying   8, 108, 121, 144, 211
turnaround   163
turnovers   142
typical 220
ubiquitous   127
ultimate   107
unable 234
unclear   33
underlying   87
undermine   121
understand   71, 145, 178, 246, 252

understood 118, 120, 146
undertake 62
underway 81
uninformed 117
unique 111, 136, 235
uniquely 241
Unless 8
unproven 201
unresolved 160, 169
updated 9-10, 73, 143, 159, 167, 179, 211-212, 223
updates 10, 99, 202, 253
updating 159
upfront 217
up-sell 112
usability 84
useful 89, 92, 155, 204
usefully 10, 24
UserID 165
utility 175
utilizing 86
vacations 142
validate 49, 250
validated 30, 40, 68, 73, 132
Validation 249
validity 146, 244
valuable 8
values 116, 209
variables 63, 93, 227
variance 6, 237, 247-248
-variance 179
variances 247-248
variation 16, 34, 59-60, 97
variations 146
variety 79
vendor 80, 131, 201, 260
vendors 17, 73, 82, 198, 259
ventilated 230
verified 10, 30, 40, 73, 132, 165, 259
verify 44, 47-51, 53-54, 92, 99, 249, 261
verifying 56
version 254, 268
versions 35, 38
versus 234

vested 111
viable 94, 154
vigorously 237
violate 153
vis-à-vis 205
vision 116, 140, 196
visualize 162, 175
voices 135
volatile 83
volatility 251
volume 247
volunteers 251
warrant 233
warranty 1, 189
weaknesses 165, 185, 213, 255
website 234
weighted 173
wellbeing 229
whether 8, 95, 125, 196, 259
-which 199, 207
widgets 186
willing 185, 208, 252
windfall 141
window 163
Windows 1-14, 16-27, 29-43, 45-103, 105-148, 150-157, 159-169, 171-187, 189, 191, 193, 195, 197-199, 201-209, 211-213, 215-217, 219-223, 225-227, 229, 232, 234, 236-237, 239, 241, 243-245, 247, 249-253, 255-259, 261, 263-266
winning 259
within 62, 89, 150, 157, 161, 193, 195, 209, 215, 221, 225, 234, 256
without 1, 12, 105, 118, 147, 213, 225, 262
workdays 204
worked 181, 199, 201, 266
workers 111
workflow 71, 228
workforce 81, 107, 109, 116
working 95, 101, 187-188, 195, 228, 251
Worksheet 4, 175, 183
worst-case 39
writing 145, 148
written 1, 159, 230
yesterday 20

youhave   144
yourself   107-108, 119, 195

Printed in Great Britain
by Amazon